The Little B

Expert Witness Practice
in the Civil Arena

The Little Book on

Expert Witness Practice
in the Civil Arena

Chris Pamplin PhD FGS
Editor
UK Register of Expert Witnesses

© 2007

J S Publications
11 Kings Court
Newmarket
Suffolk
CB8 7SG

ISBN 1-905926 00 6

First published: March 2007

Whilst the information contained herein is believed to be accurate and up to date, it is given without liability and it is for the individual to ensure compliance with the rules of court, practice directions, protocols and any codes of practice currently in effect. The information contained herein is supplied for general information purposes only and does not constitute professional advice. Neither J S Publications nor the author accept responsibility for any loss that may arise from reliance on information contained herein. You should always consult a suitably qualified advisor on any specific problem or matter.

Contents in Brief

Preface

Since 1999, the role of the expert witness working in the civil justice system in England and Wales has become increasingly complex.

In the system of case management that existed prior to 1999, lawyers held sway and the use of expert evidence as part of the case management strategy was all too common. So often this approach involved finding the most circuitous route to court; misuse of expert evidence was just one tactic adopted. So it was, perhaps, understandable that the 'hired gun' was seen from time to time.

Lord Woolf determined to stamp this out. Following the introduction of the Civil Procedure Rules in April 1999, we have seen:

- expert evidence placed under the complete control of the court
- the adoption of a cards-on-the-table approach to litigation
- absolutely clear guidance for expert witnesses on their overriding duty to the court.

But herein lies a problem for the diligent expert witness. Not only has he to be cognisant of the various rules and guidance with which he must comply, but he can no longer hide behind his instructions. His overriding duty to the court makes his position alongside the judge crystal clear; he is not an advocate for a party. Critical to the role of the expert witness is independence. And this overriding duty has made the role of expert witness an increasingly lonely one.

This book is designed as a practical guide to the complex array of rules and guidance for expert witnesses as they interact with the civil justice system in England and Wales. In recognition of the isolation borne of their independence, this book is written with the interest of the expert firmly to the fore. It encourages experts to fulfil their overriding duty to the court, and their professional duty to others, whilst making choices that protect their own interests.

Chris Pamplin

Contents in Detail

Case Index

Expert Evidence

An **expert** can be anyone with knowledge or experience of a particular field or discipline beyond that to be expected of a layman. An **expert witness** is an expert who makes this knowledge and experience available to a court[1] to help it understand the issues of a case and thereby reach a sound and just decision.

An expert witness makes knowledge available to the court

This distinction implies a further one, between advising clients and helping the court, which will be explored later (see the section on the Expert Advisor on page 29). In the meantime we will concentrate on the role and duties of an expert witness in giving or preparing evidence for the purpose of court proceedings.

What is expert evidence?

The fundamental characteristic of expert evidence is that it is **opinion** evidence. Generally speaking, lay witnesses may give only one form of evidence, namely evidence of fact. They may not say, for example, that a vehicle was being driven recklessly, only that it ended up in the ditch.

Giving expert evidence involves expressing an informed opinion

---

[1] Or other judicial and quasi-judicial bodies, e.g. tribunals, arbitrations, adjudications, select committees, official inquiries.

- It is the function of the **court** (whether judge or jury) to decide the cause of the accident based on the evidence placed before it.

An expert assists the court in reaching a just decision

- It is the task of the **expert witness** (an accident investigator, say) to assist the court in reaching its decision with technical analysis and opinion inferred from factual evidence of, for example, skid marks.

Judge needs to have confidence in expert opinion

To be truly of assistance to a court, though, expert evidence must also provide as much detail as is necessary to allow the judge (or jury[2]) to determine that the expert's opinions are well founded. It follows, then, that it will often include:

- **factual evidence obtained by the expert** which requires expertise in its interpretation and presentation
- **other factual evidence** which, while it may not require expertise for its comprehension, is inextricably linked to evidence that does
- **explanations of technical terms or topics**
- **hearsay evidence of a specialist nature**, e.g. as to the consensus of medical opinion on the causation of particular symptoms or conditions, as well as
- **opinions based on facts adduced** in the case.

When is expert evidence needed?

Experts used to extend the court's 'knowledge base'

Expert evidence is most obviously needed **when the evaluation of the issues requires technical or scientific knowledge only an expert in the field is**

---

[2] There is a general presumption for civil trials to be heard without a jury unless the court, on application, orders otherwise. The common exceptions to this are cases involving fraud, libel, slander, malicious prosecution or false imprisonment.

likely to possess. However, there is nothing in the Civil Procedure Rules (CPR) to prevent reports for court use being commissioned on any factual matter, technical or otherwise, providing:

- it is deemed likely to be **outside the knowledge and experience of those trying the case** *and*

- the **court agrees** to the evidence being called.[3]

Expert evidence in professional negligence cases

Special considerations apply when an expert is giving evidence in a case alleging professional negligence.

Professional negligence cases require extra care

In general, defendants in such cases can only be held negligent if the error complained of is not one that would have been made by a reasonably competent practitioner in the same field acting with ordinary care. There is statutory provision[4] for admitting expert opinion on whether or not that test has been satisfied. If, however, their instructions require them to express such an opinion, experts should be aware of their responsibilities in the matter.

---

[3] For the text of that part of the CPR dealing with expert evidence, see page 185. The full text of the Rules, and that of their associated practice directions and pre-action protocols, may be consulted on the website of the Department for Constitutional Affairs (DCA) at http://www.dca.gov.uk, but downloading them from there can be a tedious business. A more convenient source is **CPR Viewer**, produced by J S Publications. This is a small Windows program offering both the text and the ability to search through it simply and quickly. Contact J S Publications on (01638) 561590 for more information or surf to www.jspubs.com.

[4] Civil Evidence Act 1973, Section 3.

As Mr Justice Cresswell observed in the course of his judgment in a medical negligence case[5]:

> *'There is seldom any one answer exclusive of all others to problems of professional judgement. A court may prefer one body of opinion to another, but that is no basis for a finding of negligence...'*

He went on to observe that:

> *'An expert witness should make it clear in his/her report (if it be the case) that although the expert would have adopted a different approach or practice, he/she accepts that the [one] adopted by the defendant was in accordance with the approach or practice accepted as proper by a responsible body of practitioners skilled in the relevant field.'*

Experts must not usurp the function of the court

What experts giving evidence in professional negligence cases may not do is express an opinion, whether in their reports or under cross-examination, to the effect that: 'This happened, and therefore there was negligence'. That is a finding only the court can make.

Admissibility

Expert evidence admissible if matters at issue require expertise

Generally speaking, expert evidence is admissible whenever there are matters at issue which require expertise for their observation, analysis or description. Moreover, the courts have customarily afforded litigants wide latitude in adducing such evidence. One reason for this is that, until the evidence has been heard, the judge has little else to

---

[5] *Sharpe -v- Southend Health Authority* [1997] 8 *MedLR* 299.

go on in assessing the competence of the expert or the weight to be attached to his evidence.

Recently, though, there has been some hardening of judicial attitudes on this topic. This has been particularly so when unnecessary use of expert witnesses has resulted in delays in the hearing of cases or contributed excessively to their cost. The solution proposed by Lord Woolf in the Final Report of his inquiry into the civil justice system in England and Wales[6] was that the calling of expert evidence should be under the **complete control of the court**. The CPR, which came into force on 26 April 1999, give effect to this and many other of Lord Woolf's proposals.

Calling of expert evidence is under complete control of the court

Courts now have the power to exclude expert evidence even though it would otherwise be admissible. On the face of it, this conflicts with the right of individual litigants to present their case under conditions that do not place them at a disadvantage *vis-à-vis* their opponents – a right secured to them by the Human Rights Act 1998. Thus far, however, attempts to challenge, on human rights grounds, a court's refusal to allow parties to call the evidence they wish have met with no success (see, for example, *Daniels -v- Walker*[7]).

Court has power to exclude expert evidence even if otherwise admissible

When might expert evidence not be admissible?

There are a number of situations in which expert evidence might not be admissible. These include:

Expert evidence can be ruled out in many situations

---

[6] Access to Justice, Final Report [1996] HMSO, ISBN 0-11-380099-1.

[7] *Daniels -v- Walker* [2000] 1 *WLR* 1382.

- if the **judge considers that the expert's qualifications or experience are not sufficiently relevant** to the issues

- if, on the proven facts of the case, the **judge can form his own conclusions** without the help of expert evidence

- when it **deals with matters that are for the judge to decide**

- when the **parties themselves – as witnesses of fact – are capable of giving the evidence** themselves

- when it is **not produced in time** to enable parties to exchange reports within the timescale set by the court

- particularly in lower value claims, where obtaining the expert evidence would incur a **cost that is disproportionate to the value of the claim**

- when the **expert providing it fails to observe the requirements laid down by rules of court or practice directions** as to the form the report should take.

Court can reject evidence from hired guns

The court also has the power, of course, to reject evidence that is otherwise admissible if it should form an unfavourable view as to the impartiality of the expert providing it.

Duties of an expert witness

An expert's primary duty is to the court

The primary duty of an expert witness to the court is **to be truthful as to fact, thorough in technical reasoning, honest as to opinion and complete in coverage of relevant matters**. This applies to written reports as much as oral evidence, and regardless of whether the witness is on oath.

At the same time, when accepting instructions the expert assumes a responsibility to the client[8]:

- to **exercise due care** with regard to the investigations to be carried out, and
- to **provide opinion evidence that is soundly based**.

It is also possible that an expert will assume **professional duties of care**. In many instances, these are more onerous than those that arise from contract. These duties dictate that the expert:

Many experts assume a professional duty of care

- undertakes only those tasks he is competent to carry out, and
- gives only those opinions he is competent to provide.

To fulfil these duties adequately it is, of course, vital that the expert should also have kept up to date with current thinking and developments in his field.

Experts must keep abreast of developments

In addition, the expert must treat as confidential the identity of, and any information about, the client acquired in the course of investigations, unless their disclosure is required by law or has been authorised by the client.

Confidentiality is key

Finally, anyone accepting instructions to act as an expert witness must ensure their familiarity with the provisions of Part 35 of the CPR and the associated Practice Direction (see *Appendix 1: CPR Part 35* on page 185 and *Appendix 2: CPR Part 35 Practice Direction* on page 190). An expert should be ever mindful of the potential consequences for the client of a failure on the expert's part to observe these requirements.

Experts must comply with CPR Part 35 and its associated Practice Direction

---

[8] This is a duty that arises out of the tort of negligence.

Single joint experts

Role of SJE also governed by CPR Part 35 and the associated Practice Direction

The Single Joint Expert (SJE) owes the same overriding duty to the court as any other expert. Indeed, the role an SJE performs is governed by exactly the same provisions of CPR Part 35 and its associated Practice Direction. The SJE also owes the same duties of professional competence to the instructing parties as any expert appointed by one party alone. However, because an SJE has more than one instructing party, there is an additional requirement that in any dealings with them an SJE must conduct himself in a scrupulously fair and transparent manner. This places additional burdens on the SJE.

SJEs must be fair, open and transparent

- Each party must be kept informed of the progress being made.
- The SJE must avoid communicating with any party unilaterally.

SJEs require tact and firm resolve

There is also the possibility that one or more of the instructing parties may have wanted to instruct their own expert but were not allowed to do so by the court. If that is the case, they might well feel prejudiced. Initially, at least, they may fail to co-operate fully with the SJE whom they and their opponents have been ordered to appoint. Tact and a firm resolve are not the least of the skills required of an SJE if the role is to be fulfilled successfully.

Loneliness of the SJE

Although the primary duty of all expert witnesses is to the court, those appointed by one party alone may still have the sense of belonging to that party's team. This is especially so if they have advised on technical aspects of the case prior to the issue of proceedings.

The situation of the SJE could not be more different.

- In the great majority of instances the SJE would have had **no knowledge of the case before being appointed**, and thereafter little or no influence in determining the course it takes.

  SJEs come to a case with no prior knowledge

- Throughout the SJE's involvement he will be expected to **maintain a position of strict neutrality** *vis-à-vis* the parties, even to the extent that should one of them make contact for any reason, the SJE would be expected to ensure that the other party knows of it and has a copy of any response.

  SJEs must remain neutral

- If an SJE is required to give evidence in court, it is likely that the **instructing parties would avoid having any contact** while there. It is probable that neither side will feel in the least obliged to tell the SJE how the case is going, when the evidence is likely to be called and how long the SJE should remain in the court building.

  SJEs are isolated in court – for obvious reasons

- It is also unlikely that either of the parties will **inform the SJE subsequently of the case's outcome**.

  SJEs unlikely to be kept informed

Isolation, in a word, is a fact of life for SJEs, and not the least of its tribulations.

Qualities required of an expert witness

Expert evidence should be – and should be seen to be – independent, objective and unbiased. In particular, an expert witness must not be biased towards the party responsible for paying the fee.[9]

Experts must be independent, objective and unbiased

---

[9] The classic statement of the principles of expert evidence is that laid down by Mr Justice Cresswell in his judgment in the shipping case known as *The Ikarian Reefer*. For further details and a discussion of the 'Cresswell' principles see Appendix 4, page 212.

The evidence should be the same whoever is paying.

Clearly, too, an expert witness should have:

- a **sound knowledge of the subject matter** in dispute, and, usually, practical experience of it
- the **powers of analytical reasoning** required to fulfil the assignment
- the **ability to communicate findings and opinions** clearly, concisely and in terms adapted to the tribunal before which evidence is being given
- the **flexibility of mind to modify opinions** in the light of counter-arguments or fresh evidence
- the **ability to 'think on one's feet'**, so necessary in coping with cross-examination and re-examination.

Qualifications, training and accreditation

The court sets no pre-condition on who may appear as an expert witness

The courts do not require an expert to lay claim to any particular qualifications, training or accreditation as a prerequisite to admitting his evidence. It is enough for a party to demonstrate that the court will benefit from the proposed evidence, that it is technical evidence that would not otherwise be available to the court and that the expert possesses suitable expertise. Whilst formal qualifications will help the court in assessing an expert's expertise, the expert's professional experience will often be more relevant.

Training in the duties of an expert witness makes many experts feel more confident in their interactions with lawyers and the courts. There are numerous commercial training companies that offer courses. The various expert witness bodies, such as the

Society of Expert Witnesses[10], also offer
conferences and workshops.

Formal systems of accreditation for expert witnesses
were given a boost by the formation of the Council
for the Registration of Forensic Practitioners (CRFP),
and the proposal contained in a Legal Services
Commission consultation paper[11] that all experts
paid out of public funds should be registered with
CRFP. However, the Civil Justice Council (CJC) has
concluded[12] that mandatory accreditation of expert
witnesses is neither possible nor desirable. Instead,
the CJC has pronounced that professional
organisations and expert bodies should work
together to implement high standards and follow
principles of accreditation on which a broad
consensus can be reached.

Mandatory accreditation of experts as witnesses has been ruled to be unworkable

Ethical considerations

The duties an expert witness owes to the court may
sometimes run counter to those owed to the client.
This will be most obviously so when the expert's
conclusions contradict the client's case as set out in
the pleadings. In such circumstances the expert
witness may come under pressure to alter the report
or suppress the damaging opinion. To do either
would be tantamount to committing perjury, while not
to do so might well undermine the client's case.
There are only two ways in which such an issue can
be resolved: either the statement of case is amended
or the expert witness must withdraw.

Expert must never alter opinion to accommodate client

---

[10] See http://www.sew.org.uk.

[11] The Use of Experts, November 2004. See
http://www.jspubs.com/downloads/PDFs/LSCNov04.pdf.

[12] See http://www.jspubs.com/downloads/PDFs/CJC_EFII_a.pdf.

Experts must never ignore damaging information

An expert witness can never afford to ignore information damaging to the client's case once it comes to light, if only because there is always the risk that the other side will become aware of it too. In any event, the expert's duty to the court requires that his evidence is **complete in its coverage** of relevant matters.

Experts must never apportion blame

Lastly, an expert should never express any opinion on allegations of negligence on the part of anyone, professional or otherwise, who may be involved in a dispute. The opinions given should relate solely to the facts of the case: it is for others to apportion blame.

Conflicts of interest

Financial

Experts must never accept payment that is contingent on the outcome of a case

Expert witnesses have a duty to the court to be independent and objective in the evidence they provide. Judges may, in the exercise of their discretion, reject altogether evidence tendered by experts whom they know to have – or suspect of having – a financial stake in the outcome of the litigation. This is the principal reason why experts should **never** accept instructions to act as an expert witness on a 'no-win, no-fee' basis.

It should also be remembered that the Law Society of England and Wales specifically states at 21.11 of its *Guide to the Professional Conduct of Solicitors* that:

> '*A solicitor must not make or offer to make payments to a witness contingent upon the nature of the evidence given or upon the outcome of a case*'.

Pre-existing links

For much the same reason, personal, professional or financial links with parties to a dispute, or with businesses in competition with them, will properly be the subject of detailed scrutiny. A link does not create an automatic bar to an expert acting as an expert witness in any litigation in which those parties are engaged, but it does need to be disclosed to the parties and the court.

Any links with litigating parties must be declared

In the case of *Liverpool Roman Catholic Archdiocesan Trustees Inc -v- Goldberg*[13] the claimant was suing a QC, alleging negligence in advice he had given on a tax matter. At a case management conference the procedural judge gave both parties permission to call expert evidence from a tax barrister, and the defendant chose to instruct another QC from his own chambers. In his report the colleague clearly stated that the defendant was a friend whom he had known for 28 years.

Reports were exchanged in November 1999 and no question was raised about the admissibility of that prepared by the defendant's expert until January 2002. By this time the date fixed for trial was only 2 months away. At that stage the claimant applied to the High Court for a ruling that the report be excluded on the grounds that:

- its author could not be independent, and
- independence was necessary for an expert's evidence to be received.

When this matter finally reached the Court of Appeal it was as a commentary in the reserved judgment in

Ideally experts should have no interest in the outcome of the proceedings

---

[13] *Liverpool Roman Catholic Archdiocesan Trustees Inc -v- Goldberg* [2001] 1 *AER* 182.

the *Factortame No. 8* case[14]. The Master of the Rolls said that while it is always desirable that an expert should have no actual or apparent interest in the outcome of the proceedings in which he gives evidence, such disinterest is not automatically a precondition to the admissibility of the expert evidence. If an expert should have an interest of one kind or another, the question of whether that expert may be permitted to give evidence should be determined in the course of case management. The judge will then have to weigh up the alternatives open to him if the expert evidence is to be excluded, bearing in mind the overriding objective of doing justice for the parties.

This case supports the earlier judgment in *Field -v- Leeds City Council*[15] concerning a claim by tenants against their local authority landlord in respect of alleged disrepair. Leeds City Council, the defendant, wished to call a surveyor, employed by them in their Claims Investigation Section, as an expert witness. The district judge refused to entertain this evidence on the ground that the expert was not independent. On appeal, the circuit judge upheld this decision.

But the Court of Appeal unanimously agreed that a surveyor employed by the Council was not, for that reason alone, automatically disqualified from giving expert evidence on its behalf. As Lord Justice Waller observed, whether he should be able to do so depended on whether it could be demonstrated that he had the relevant expertise and was mindful of his primary duty to the court.

---

[14] *R (Factortame Ltd & Others) -v- Secretary of State for Transport, Local Government and the Regions (No. 8)* [2002] *EWCA Civ* 932.

[15] *Field -v- Leeds City Council* [2000] 17 *EG* 165.

Former clients

Expert witnesses need to be particularly mindful of the risks involved in acting in cases involving former clients. Allegations could arise that knowledge or information gained while working for the former client is being used to the new client's advantage.

Whenever there is a conflict of interest of this kind, or it appears that there may be one, the expert concerned should seek to obtain the informed consent of both the old and the new client before agreeing to act for the latter.

Experts should beware cases involving former clients

This may not be as straightforward as it sounds. It will involve – at the very least – disclosing to each client the other's name and the nature of the assignment completed or envisaged.

As a first step, then, it would be necessary for the expert to clear with each client what he proposes to tell the other. In securing the former client's consent, it may help if the expert has returned all the papers relating to the case or cases in which evidence was given on behalf of the former client. If that client's consent should not be forthcoming, however, the expert ought to decline to be instructed in the new case.

Experts must seek agreement of all parties before accepting case

How to handle a potential conflict of interest

The Court of Appeal – in *Toth -v- Jarman*[16] – has given guidance on how expert witnesses should handle potential conflicts of interest.

This was an appeal by a claimant in a clinical negligence claim. The defendant was a general practitioner who treated the claimant's son. Despite treatment, the son died and the claimant sought

---

[16] *Toth -v- Jarman* [2006] *EWCA Civ* 1028.

damages for psychiatric injury based on the defendant's alleged negligence. The Medical Defence Union (MDU) was acting for the defendant and instructed an expert to report. The expert's evidence was favourable to the defendant, and at trial it was preferred by the judge to the claimant's expert's evidence. However, on appeal, the claimant said there had been material non-disclosure by the expert of a conflict of interest arising out of the fact that the expert was a member of the Cases Committee of the MDU at the time the report was written. The Cases Committee is the part of the MDU that takes decisions on whether to defend any given action.

The Court of Appeal said that a conflict of interest does not automatically disqualify an expert from giving evidence. The key is whether the expert's opinion is independent of the parties and the pressures of the litigation. A party that wishes to call an expert with a potential conflict of interest should disclose details of that conflict at as early a stage in the proceedings as possible so that the other party and the court can properly assess the conflict of interest.

It was not enough for the defence to say the claimant hadn't asked about the expert's relationship with the MDU. If there was a conflict of interest that was 'not obviously immaterial', it should have been disclosed by the expert to her instructing solicitors and from them to the claimant's solicitors.

However, in rejecting the appeal, the Court of Appeal said the practice of the Cases Committee of the MDU to exclude an expert involved in the litigation from discussions about the case meant that membership of the Committee would not automatically disqualify that expert from being an expert witness. Furthermore, the expert had, in fact, ceased to be a member of the Committee 6 months before the trial. In the circumstances, even if the expert's conflict of interest had been a disqualifying interest initially, it had then become 'immaterial', and so there was no basis for interfering with the judge's decision.

Guidance for experts

The Court of Appeal then went on to consider what should happen in any similar future situation.

> *'The expert should not leave undisclosed any conflict of interest which might bring into question the suitability of his evidence as the basis for the court's decision. The conflict of interest could be of any kind, including a financial interest, a personal connection, or an obligation, for example, as a member or officer of some other body. But ultimately, the question of what conflicts of interest fall within this description is a question for the court, taking into account all the circumstances of the case.*

Experts must report conflicts of interest immediately

> *'Without wishing to be over-prescriptive or to limit consideration by the Civil Procedure Rules Committee, we are of the view that consideration should be given to requiring an expert to make a statement at the end of his report on the following lines:*

> *(a) that he has no conflict of interest of any kind, other than any which he has disclosed in his report;*

> *(b) that he does not consider that any interest which he has disclosed affects his suitability as an expert witness on any issue on which he has given evidence;*

(c) that he will advise the party by whom he is instructed if, between the date of his report and the trial, there is any change in circumstances which affects his answers to (a) or (b) above.

'As we see it, a form of declaration to this effect should assist in reminding both the expert and the party calling him of the need to inform the other parties and the court of any possible conflict of interest.'

Experts should include additional signed declaration

However, there appears to be an inconsistency in what the Court of Appeal has said about a party not needing to notify the court or the opposition of an 'obviously immaterial' conflict of interest, when the proposed expert's declaration contains no such qualification. Hopefully the Civil Procedure Rules Committee will refine the wording of the declaration on its passage into the Rules. For now, though, experts ought to adopt the form of words suggested by the Court of Appeal.

Roles of the expert

The number of roles an expert might taken on has grown significantly under the CPR. When advising a party, but there is no intention of putting the expert's opinions before the court, the expert is known as an **expert advisor**. If the expert advisor is working 'behind the scenes' in a claim before the courts, the term **shadow expert** is often used instead. An expert instructed by just one party in a claim, and whose opinion is to be put before the court, is an **expert witness** proper. If the expert witness is instructed by all the parties in a claim, then the **single joint expert** epithet applies. In a complex claim, involving many experts, one expert witness may be appointed the **lead expert**. Finally, the CPR also introduced the role of a truly court-appointed expert. Known as an **assessor**, this type of expert appointment is seldom seen in practice.

Expert advisor

The great majority of civil cases are settled before they reach court. With many of them the role of expert may go no further than investigating the circumstances and providing the instructing solicitor with an interim report or assessment of the technical strength of the client's case. Such reports will often be used by the lawyer as a 'bargaining chip' in the negotiation that takes place with the other side.

Most expert reports used as bargaining chips to settle claims

If the expert is involved before the case has actually begun, i.e. before the statement of claim has been served, the expert may be considered to be an 'advisory' expert, rather than an expert witness. This status has important ramifications for the expert as it removes any claim to immunity against civil suit the expert may later wish to assert (see *Immunity* on page 159).

Experts involved pre-litigation are advisors and not immune from suit

Expert witness

The expert's duties may be extended greatly if it should be decided to proceed to trial. The expert may then be expected to advise on:

It is important to recognise when the role changes

- the **technical matters averred in the statement of case**
- the **technical content of requests for further particulars** (or the responses to such requests), and
- the **technical significance of evidence disclosed** by the opposing side.

The expert may also be asked to produce a report for use in court.

Expert writing report

29

Expert attending meeting of experts

Furthermore, after reports have been exchanged, the expert will probably be asked for an assessment of the report prepared by the expert for the opposing side. He may also be required to attend meetings of experts with a view to narrowing issues still in dispute (see *Meetings of Experts*, page 93).

Expert undergoing cross-examination

Expert offering technical support

During the trial an expert will not only have to face cross-examination on his own evidence, but be on hand to advise counsel about weaknesses to be probed in that of the opposing side's expert (see *The Report*, page 61). Finally, the expert may be required to provide further technical support should the case go to appeal.

It can be seen that an expert can have several distinct roles to play in litigation, that these roles will overlap in time and that they may extend over the duration of a case, from inception to appeal. Being an expert witness is not simply a case of writing reports – it can involve much else besides.

2 Instructions

The giving and taking of instructions lies at the heart of the solicitor–expert relationship. It is, then, surprising that:

Experts and lawyers need to communicate well if problems are to be avoided

- many lawyers appear to assume that all experts understand what is needed, and
- many experts assume that lawyers will automatically provide everything required for the instruction to proceed smoothly.

Alas, the world of the expert witness is not that ordered!

Advice or report?

First, and most obviously, the solicitor must be clear about why expert help is required.

- Is it, perhaps, that an appraisal is needed of the technical issues presented by the case before the solicitor can decide whether or not to undertake it, possibly on a conditional fee basis?
- Is help needed in early attempts to negotiate settlement of a dispute?
- Is help required in framing the client's statement of case and to identify weaknesses in that of the opponent?

Expert advisor owes duty to instructing party

An expert acting in an **advisory role** such as these is beholden to his instructing party and no one else. That party alone decides whether and for what purpose the expert's services are likely to prove useful.

Expert advisor not immune from suit

In this pre-action setting, the expert is an 'advisory expert', not an 'expert witness'. The expert is acting as a **professional advisor**. This means that the expert will be open to any subsequent claim in negligence for this advice that may arise (see *Immunity* on page 159 for more details).

Expert witness duties stipulated by CPR

It is a different matter if the solicitor envisages needing an expert to **prepare evidence for use in court**. In that event the CPR come into play, and they stipulate (among other things) that:

- no party may call an expert or put in evidence an expert's report without the **court's permission** [r.35.4(1)]
- it is the duty of an expert to **help the court** on the matters within his expertise and that duty overrides any obligation to the party instructing or paying the expert [r.35.3(1)], and
- an expert's report must state the **substance of all material instructions**, whether written or oral, on the basis of which the report was written [r.35.10(3)].

These requirements are fundamental in determining how solicitors can and should instruct experts to prepare evidence for use in court proceedings.

Authority to instruct

Obtaining authority of the paying party

Who is paying the bill?

Yet another important consideration for the solicitor is that of who, ultimately, will be responsible for meeting the expert's costs, whether the whole amount or part thereof.

Generally speaking, a solicitor is personally liable to pay the 'proper costs' of any expert he may instruct. If the solicitor instructs an expert for his own purposes, e.g. to conduct a risk assessment of a case, the expert's fees would, of course, have to be met by the solicitor's firm. It is more likely, though, that the solicitor will be engaging the services of an expert on behalf of a client. In such circumstances the solicitor will want to ensure that the necessary authority to instruct has been gained from either the client or any third party that may be funding the litigation, e.g. the client's insurers or the Legal Services Commission. Without that authority the solicitor may experience difficulty later on in getting fully reimbursed for the expenditure incurred.[1]

Solicitor personally liable for expert fees

Obtaining permission of the court

If the expert's help is needed to prepare evidence for use in court, the solicitor has a further hurdle to surmount: how to convince the procedural judge in charge of the case that:

Procedural judge will need convincing that expert report is required

- the **evidence is necessary** to prove the facts alleged by the client, or
- the expert's **opinion would be helpful** to the court in deciding the case at trial.

Provided the judge accepts the solicitor's arguments on this point, he may then want to hear why the evidence or opinion cannot be provided by a single expert appointed jointly by the parties. Only if the judge allows evidence to be submitted by experts that have been separately appointed would it be safe

SJE preferred wherever possible

---

[1] For further information on these topics see *Chapter 7: Payment of Fees* and *The Little Book on Expert Fees* published by J S Publications (see *www.jspubs.com/LittleBooks*).

for the solicitor to instruct one of his own volition. This is because, unless the judge agrees to separate ('party appointed') experts, the solicitor will be unable to recover from the other party any costs incurred in such an instruction.

Locating the expert

Solicitors have a duty to locate the right expert quickly

Let us assume that the solicitor has the client's authority to instruct an expert and, where necessary, the court's permission to adduce expert evidence. Now follows the task of locating an expert with the experience and expertise appropriate to the complexity and importance of the case.

Unless the solicitor has previously handled cases of a similar nature, or is familiar with the subject matter of the litigation, finding that expert may not be all that easy. Yet a case can be lost by default if the right expert is not found quickly. This is, of course, why so many solicitors turn for help to the *UK Register of Expert Witnesses*.[2]

Just as a householder will follow a predictable course in selecting a good plumber, so lawyers tend to follow a well-worn path in tracking down an expert. In approximate order of preference they use:

- their personal experience of an expert
- a close colleague's experience of an expert
- an expert in the law firm's database
- a recommendation by a professional colleague
- a recommendation by a client
- a professional expert body
- one of the directories.

[2] *UK Register of Expert Witnesses* website: www.jspubs.com, telephone (01638) 561590.

This process has, however, been circumvented in the case of low-value, high-volume personal injury cases. In these, medico-legal reporting organisations have tended to take over the task of locating and dealing with experts – to the detriment of the expert, lawyer and claimant alike.

Assessing the marketing opportunities

When the *UK Register of Expert Witnesses* was first published back in 1988 the options for experts seeking to promote their availability as expert witnesses were limited. As the marketplace has grown it has become increasingly more time-consuming for experts to gain a proper understanding of the various directories and expert witness bodies they might join. (If spending hours trawling through the various websites doesn't sound like fun, then you can use the J S Publications *Comparator Grid*[3] to get a feel for what is on offer. Simply select the features most important to you, and the *Comparator Grid* will show you how everyone fares.)

Experts now faced with a confusing raft of advertising opportunities

How a solicitor assesses an expert

Once a shortlist of experts has been identified, the next task for the solicitor is to decide which expert to choose. For each expert, this will involve:

- considering the qualifications, CV and brochure to ensure the expert is suitable and able to communicate this through his background and promotional material
- following up any references provided
- looking at the quality, or even existence, of appropriate Terms of Engagement as these will help to reassure the solicitor that the

---

[3] Browse to *www.jspubs.com/Experts/comp/*

expert is properly organised to take on instructions

- finding out how many instructions the expert has received to date and, even though it should be of no relevance in an expert who owes a primary duty to the court, the balance between claimant, defendant and SJE work

- ascertaining what proportion of the expert's working week is spent on expert witness work. Some solicitors prefer an expert who still has current professional involvement in the claimed area of expertise, although the court's timetabling policy works against such experts offering their services.

Initial enquiry

Initial enquiries confirm case detail, availability, expertise and funding

Once a suitable expert has been located, the solicitor's next step is to contact the expert direct. The solicitor will need to

- **outline the matter** on which assistance is required

- confirm the **appropriateness** of the expert's expertise by exploring how the experience and qualifications of the expert mesh with the issue under investigation

- establish the expert's **availability and resources** for undertaking the assignment, and

- check that there are no potential **conflicts of interest**.

Expertise confirmed in CV

All this can be done by letter, of course, but it is more likely that an initial enquiry of this kind will be made by telephone. The solicitor may go on to ask for a CV confirming the expert's experience, academic qualifications and professional training appropriate to the assignment. At this point, too, the solicitor ought to make clear how the litigation is being funded, e.g. Legal Services Commission, private client, etc.

Single joint experts

Ideally the solicitors jointly appointing an SJE will have agreed in advance:

Ideally solicitors should agree instructions and lead solicitor in advance

- the **instructions** to be given and
- **which party is to liaise** with the SJE direct (the lead solicitor).

So sorting out queries arising from the instructions received should prove no more difficult than for a party-appointed expert, although in the nature of things it may take a little longer to achieve. Nevertheless, the SJE should copy to the solicitors for the other parties any queries about the instructions that were addressed to the lead solicitor. Doing so should not only help to secure a speedier response but also serve to show all parties that the SJE intends keeping them fully in the picture.

Experts should keep all parties fully informed

The real problems begin when the parties fail to agree the SJE's instructions and choose instead to instruct the SJE independently. Rule 35.8(2) provides that in such circumstances each party giving instructions must at the same time copy them to the other parties. By then, though, the damage will have been done.

When solicitors can't work together, experts suffer

Separate sets of instructions almost inevitably require some reconciling, and the expert will need to let the parties know how this is to be achieved. If it involves carrying out more test procedures than any of the parties had envisaged, the SJE should alert them to the fact that more expense will be incurred as a result.

Separate sets of instructions need reconciling and increase costs

If, however, the separate instructions require the SJE to make different assumptions of fact, then difficulties

If asked to assume different sets of facts, more than one set of opinions required	could begin to multiply alarmingly. In such circumstances there may be no alternative but to produce a report that provides more than one set of opinions on the issue in question, depending on the assumptions the SJE has been instructed to make. It will then be up to the court to decide which set of assumptions it prefers and therefore which set of opinions it can accept.
Conflicting demands increase cost	The SJE should take care to ensure that all the parties are fully aware that by making conflicting demands they are increasing the cost of the report required by the court.
Ultimate recourse: seek direction from court or resign appointment	In extreme cases, it may be that the separate instructions an SJE receives differ so fundamentally that there is no way in which a report can be produced that embraces them all. In that event, the SJE will need to consider whether further directions should be sought from the court (in accordance with CPR 35.14) or the appointment should be resigned altogether. If the parties allow either to happen, however, they risk incurring the displeasure of the court and being penalised for it as to costs. Accordingly, the mere threat of taking such action may be enough to get the parties to revise their instructions and make them easier to carry out.

Getting at the information

Parties can be reluctant to release material	Parties instructing an SJE, whether jointly or separately, may not co-operate with the SJE as whole-heartedly as they might. Nowhere is this more apparent than in the reluctance they can show in releasing all the information the SJE thinks may be needed to carry out the assignment.
As a last resort, experts can ask the court to intervene	Here again, the SJE has the option of seeking the court's help to resolve the problem. But it is one that should be exercised only as a last resort – as, for

example, when all the parties are proving equally unco-operative. In other circumstances, an altogether better method of proceeding is for the expert to send the party that appears to be withholding information a firm letter setting out exactly why it is needed. As always, a copy of the letter should go to the solicitors for the other parties. In other words, leave it to them to sort matters out.

At the end of the day, an SJE should only prepare a report for the court:

- if satisfied that all the information required to form an opinion has been supplied, or
- if the instructing parties have agreed that the report may be written without the additional information requested by the SJE.

In the latter circumstance, of course, the SJE must qualify the opinion given in the report and state why it was necessary to do so. It will then be up to the court to draw the inferences it chooses from the action of the party, or parties, in withholding the information in the first place.

What if material is withheld with party agreement?

Expert's response

There are various ways in which an expert can respond to a solicitor's initial enquiry. It might be, of course, that the expert lacks the appropriate expertise, is simply not available to carry out the assignment outlined, or is not interested in undertaking it. If that is the case, the expert should say so straightaway.

If unable to accept instruction, say so immediately

Assuming, though, that the expert is both available and interested, the initial response to the enquiry could prove crucial to a satisfactory outcome.

If the expert has worked for the solicitor before and on that previous occasion the solicitor behaved

Always confirm willingness to assist in writing, including terms of engagement

impeccably, there may be no harm in expressing there and then a willingness to assist again – subject, that is, to the **expert's** usual **terms of engagement**. Even so, it is always wise to follow up any verbal expression of willingness with a letter to both confirm this and either incorporating the expert's terms or attaching a copy of them.

It is absolutely essential that an expert adopts this procedure if:

- it is the first time he has been approached by anyone from the law firm, or
- the expert is less than happy with the way in which he was treated previously by the firm.

Willingness to assist is not acceptance of instructions

In no sense does 'willingness to assist' imply commitment to do so – that comes only after:

- the expert's terms have been agreed
- the expert has been fully instructed, and
- the expert has accepted the instructions.

Terms of engagement are dealt with more fully in another book in this series[4], but it is pertinent to repeat the warning given there about the weasel words some solicitors use when asked to confirm their acceptance of terms. They may, for example, 'acknowledge receipt' of an expert's terms or state that they 'understand' them. Both expressions fall a long way short of what is needed.

Design terms such that lawyers must sign a printed form with your wording of acceptance

To obviate the risk of wily solicitors devising statements of 'acceptance' along these lines, some experts prefer to enclose with their terms of engagement a printed form for solicitors to sign and return which confirms acceptance in words of the expert's own choosing.

---

[4] For more on terms of engagement for expert witnesses see *The Little Book on Expert Fees* (see *www.jspubs.com/LittleBooks*).

At this stage, too, the expert should seek to establish the kind of assistance the solicitor requires, i.e. whether it is advice **or** the preparation of evidence for use in court – if not already apparent.[5] Ultimately, of course, the expert's help may be sought for both purposes. But it is as well for them to be clearly distinguished from the outset. While instructions for advice are privileged against disclosure, those requiring the preparation of evidence are not.

Privilege attaches to instructions for expert advice

Then again, if the solicitor has not already volunteered the information, the expert should enquire how and by whom the fees and expenses are to be paid.

Experts should confirm paymaster

- If the solicitor needs **expert advice** to decide whether to take on a case, then the cost of obtaining it is a **business overhead of the law firm** and it alone would be responsible for paying the expert's bill.
- In other circumstances it is more likely that the cost is to be borne by the client, the client's insurers or the Legal Services Commission. Then the expert should seek assurance that the solicitor has obtained **prior authority** to engage his services. If this prior authority is lacking, the relevant party might refuse to reimburse the solicitor for the charges the expert makes. That could be the beginning of a long drawn-out battle to get paid.

Prior authority from paymaster essential

Initial briefing

The overriding objective of the CPR is to enable courts to deal with cases justly, and that includes dealing with them in ways proportionate to the value of the claim. This objective also applies to the

Lawyers can be penalised if court considers unreasonable costs incurred

---

[5] For further discussion of the importance of this distinction, see *Chapter 9: Immunity from Suit.*

lawyers in such cases. The court has the power to deny them full recovery of their costs if it deems any part of those costs to have been incurred unreasonably.

Lawyers will seek to minimise cost of experts

It follows that lawyers will generally seek to minimise the expense of instructing experts where possible. So in straightforward cases lawyers frequently choose to brief their chosen experts by letter or telephone. If the matter is at all complex, though, instruction may have to be done face to face. Either way, the lawyer needs to explain the dispute in sufficient depth for the expert to understand the issues to be addressed. It is, after all, much easier to frame the answer to a question if one understands the context in which it is being asked.

Initial briefing should inform, clarify and confirm

An initial briefing of this kind should:

- establish for the expert those matters the solicitor regards as relevant to the outcome of the case
- give the expert the opportunity to make clear any aspect of the assignment with which he may be unfamiliar, is not qualified to tackle, or for which the assistance of others might be required.

Estimates

Provide a cost estimate

It is at this juncture that the question of cost is most likely to arise. Even if the lawyer does not ask for an estimate, it is always prudent to provide one.

Subdivide estimate into assignment stages and show workings clearly

Assuming the expert charges an hourly rate, the estimate should itemise the time each stage of the assignment is expected to take. By simple multiplication and addition, the total fee likely to be charged by the end of the case should be clearly stated.

Travelling time may be included for the purposes of this calculation. However, the actual expense of air, rail or taxi fares should always be reckoned, and ultimately charged for, at cost, along with any other disbursements the expert anticipates incurring while carrying out the assignment.

Travel fares should be charged at cost

There are three other points concerning estimates that are worth bearing in mind. The first is that if an estimate has been computed on the basis of an hourly rate, the expert providing it must keep a record of:

Keep an accurate time sheet record

- the **amount of time each day** that he spends on the assignment, and

- the **nature of the work** undertaken.

This worksheet should then be submitted with the expert's invoice. Even though the amount of time it records may be less than that estimated initially, the instructing solicitor could be required to produce it when the court comes to assess the costs of the case.

Submit worksheet with invoice to aid cost assessment

Remember that estimates are never binding. However, experts do need to inform their instructing solicitor if it should ever become apparent that they have underestimated the time it will take to complete a job or the expenses they will be incurring along the way. The solicitor's authority to continue should always be sought.

If estimate too low, inform solicitor and seek authority to continue

Finally, there is no reason why invoices for expert witness work should not be submitted in stages, especially if the case is proceeding to trial. In any event, most experts submit an invoice with their final report, whether or not the case is expected to go further.

Submit staged invoices as case proceeds

Clarity

Poor instructions lead to increased costs

It should go without saying that solicitors ought to provide clear instructions, but sadly they do not always do so. Sometimes this is through incompetence; more often it stems from slipshod thinking. Whatever the reason, a failure to instruct properly is likely to result in an expert report that is unfocused or inadequate in other ways. As a result, the report may require considerable reworking before it can be submitted to the court or exchanged with the other side – and all at the client's expense.

Insist on precise written instructions, not wishy-washy phrasing

An expert should be particularly wary of instructions that call on him to investigate 'any other issues you may consider relevant'. Such phrases open up the possibility of recriminations later on, should the expert omit to cover an issue that turns out to be crucial to the outcome of the case. This is why the expert should always insist on having written instructions, or at any rate written confirmation of any instructions given verbally, before work commences. This applies regardless of whether the expert has met previously with the solicitor to discuss the matter.

Sit back and think carefully – What else needs confirming?

An expert needs the opportunity written instructions afford to reflect on the technical issues the case presents and to let the solicitor know if there is any other information required to carry out the assignment. Likely questions arising will include:

- Are there **witness statements** to be seen, or **reports** from experts who have been instructed to deal with other aspects of the case?

- If proceedings have already been issued, can a copy of the **statement of claim** be provided?

- What of the **other documents** in the case, e.g. medical records?
- Is **permission needed to visit the site/examine the patient**, and, if so, has this been obtained?

The main requirement for instructions is that they should be specific and unambiguous. The amount of detail they provide will depend on the type of case and the frequency with which the solicitor has instructed the expert in the past.

Specific, unambiguous instructions essential

Objectivity

Clients often have difficulty coming to terms with the idea that the expert for whom they are paying is not someone who will go into court and argue their position, come what may. For their part, solicitors need to be sensitive to this. Clients must be convinced that only unbiased expert evidence will do their case any good. It is still more important, though, to ensure that the expert fully understands the need for objectivity in his reports and in any evidence given from the witness box.

Hired guns not in anyone's interest – least of all the client's

Letter of instruction

Before the CPR came into force in April 1999 it was generally held that all communications between a solicitor and the experts instructed on a client's behalf were privileged from disclosure. That position was substantially altered by the new requirement that an expert's report must state 'the substance' of the instructions received [CPR 35.10(3)].

Experts must state the substance of their instructions

As a result, solicitors are now having to take much greater care in framing the written instructions they give their experts. Indeed, it is unlikely to help the client if the court should perceive these to be subjectively slanted. Quite apart from the sanctions

Greater care now required of solicitors in framing written instructions

the court may impose on that count, there is also the risk that it may refuse to allow the client to rely on any part of the expert's report.

Minimum requirements

Requirements of a letter of instruction

The solicitor's letter of instruction should at the very least state:

(i) the **party** for whom the solicitor is acting and whether the solicitor is seeking to appoint an expert on behalf of that party alone or jointly with the other party to the dispute (in which event the expert will also need to know when and how to contact that other party)

(ii) the sort of **assistance required**, i.e. a report for advice only or one for use in court

(iii) the precise kind of **expertise** called for

(iv) an **outline history** of the matter, identifying any factual aspects that are in dispute

(v) the **assumed facts**, i.e. those the expert is not required to investigate, often because they are agreed by the other party

(vi) the **issues** on which the expert's opinion is being sought

(vii) details of **relevant documents** to be supplied by the solicitor on acceptance of instructions, and whether these will need to be returned to the solicitor in due course

(viii) **whether proceedings have started**, and, if so, in which court and to which track the case has been allocated and whether the court has issued any directions with regard to expert evidence

(ix) any **time constraints** on the provision of advice or the submission of reports – and, if proceedings have started, the date(s) fixed for the hearing

(x) **basic information** such as contact names, addresses and telephone numbers.

It is also desirable for the solicitor to disclose the approximate value of the claim and the names of any other experts already instructed in the case.

Experts should raise queries about instruction early in the legal process

It is in the interests of all concerned that the expert should raise at this stage any queries about the instructions received. The solicitor should respond promptly to requests for clarification. It is important, too, that before accepting instructions the expert should make it clear if there is any aspect of the assignment:

- with which he is unfamiliar

- with which he is not qualified to deal, or

- that requires the assistance of others to carry it out.

Above all, an expert should **never accept instructions if there is any uncertainty** as to whether he will be able to complete the assignment within a reasonable time or according to any timetable the court may have set for the exchange of expert reports. Similarly, an expert should not agree to be instructed in a case for which a court appearance will be required if there is any likelihood that he will not be available to give evidence when the case comes to trial. Since the CPR came into force, courts have shown a marked reluctance to change the dates of hearings to suit the convenience of parties or their experts once the dates have been set.

Accept the case only if you can meet with all timetabling commitments

Assistance required

In most cases, letters of instruction will go no further than requesting a report. But experts should be aware that once the report has been provided it may not be the end of their involvement.

Submission of report may not be the end of expert involvement

The majority of civil cases are settled before they reach court, and the remainder will mostly be assigned to the fast track (where written expert evidence alone is admissible). But those worth more than £15,000 could be allocated to the multi-track. If that happens, the expert may eventually be required to give evidence from the witness box and be cross-examined on it.

In other circumstances the expert may be asked simply to investigate the matter in dispute and to provide a preliminary report to assess the strength of the client's case. Should that result in the matter being taken no further, there will be nothing more for the expert to do.

Role of the expert can evolve throughout a case

Between these two extremes there is a host of ways in which an expert might become involved.

- The request for a preliminary report could well be followed by one for a full report destined for exchange with the other side and possible use in court.
- The expert might be asked to take part in a meeting of experts with a view to narrowing the issues in dispute and negotiating a settlement.
- The expert could be called upon to advise on the technical matters within his expertise to be averred in pleadings, the technical content of requests for further and better particulars (or the response to such requests) and the technical significance of documents disclosed

by the other side – as well as to produce the draft and final versions of a full report.

- After reports have been exchanged, the expert may well be asked for a technical assessment of the report prepared by the expert for the opposition.

- At trial, the expert may be asked to advise counsel on the weaknesses to be probed in cross-examination.

- Finally, the expert may be required to provide further technical back-up should the case go to appeal.

As can be seen, expert witnesses can have several roles to play in litigation, and there are many permutations of these roles. The potential extent of an expert's involvement in a case may well not be apparent from the instructions received at the outset.

Acceptance of instructions

If, after receiving instructions and clarifying any details of doubt, the expert is prepared to accept the assignment, acceptance should always be confirmed in writing. To avoid any possibility of confusion it would be as well for the expert to use this opportunity to:

Confirm acceptance in writing

- set out his **understanding** of the issues to be covered in the report(s)

- give a **timetable** for producing the report(s)

- specify whatever **other information** may be required before a start can be made

- confirm that no conflicts of interest have been identified, and

- confirm the task is within his expertise.

Provision of documents

Any document or instruction of any relevance must be referenced

The solicitor's letter of instruction should have listed the documents in his possession that will be sent to the expert on acceptance of the assignment. Under the duty imposed by the CPR[6] an expert witness must provide a summary of all material instructions. This means that any document, or verbal instruction, of any relevance to the opinion the expert forms will need to be referenced in the written report.

Beware of documents for 'background' use only

An expert should be particularly alert to any attempt by the solicitor, when forwarding a document, to claim that it is provided for background only and should not be relied upon by the expert or mentioned in any report prepared for exchange or use in court. **If a document is material to the expert's opinion it must be referenced in the report.** (See the section on privilege starting on page 53 for a fuller discussion of this point.)

Medical records require consent for disclosure

In the case of medical records, it may be that these are still held by the hospital or the client's general practitioner. In this case it is possible that the expert may have to apply to see them. At the very least, though, the solicitor should be able to state where the records are located and provide evidence that the client/patient has given consent for their disclosure.

Solicitor should forward relevant disclosed documents immediately

In general, the solicitor should respond promptly to any requests from the expert for further information, the need for which may become apparent in the course of the investigations. Without prompting, the solicitor ought also to send copies of all documents, witness statements, pleadings, etc., disclosed by the

---

[6] c.f. CPR PD 2.2(3) (page 190) and CJC *Experts Protocol* 13.15 (page 204).

other side that may have a bearing on the issues on which the expert will be reporting.[7]

Finally, on exchange of reports, the solicitor has a duty to inform the expert when exchange took place and to send a copy of the report prepared by the expert for the other side. The latter is essential because it:

- may reveal information or raise issues that might make the expert wish to change an opinion expressed in his report, or

- may prompt a rejoinder in the form of a supplementary report.

As a matter of courtesy, the solicitor ought also to keep the expert posted on the progress of the action, including any amendments to the pleadings that are relevant to the expert's opinion. Experience shows this to be a duty more often observed in the breach!

Solicitors should keep experts appraised of case progress

Reception of the expert's report

As noted previously, instructing solicitors will usually ask their expert witnesses to submit reports intended for exchange in draft form (see *Chapter 3 The Report* for a detailed discussion of the expert report). The purpose of this is not, as some might suppose, to have the expert alter it better to support the client's case. It is to ensure that:

Experts asked to submit draft report first

- the report **meets the requirements of the court** (to which, in any case, it has to be addressed), and in particular those requirements as to its content which are

[7] For an example of the dire consequences of failure to do this experts in the *UK Register of Expert Witnesses* can see *Alan Clark -v- Associated Newspapers Ltd* on page 5 of *Your Witness 13* (*www.jspubs.com/experts/library/lib_ywidx.cfm*).

specified in the CPR and relevant practice directions, and

- the report is **organised in a way that will facilitate the examination-in-chief of the expert**, should a court appearance subsequently be required.

Does the report fulfil the brief and comply with the CPR?

With these considerations in mind, the aspects of the report on which the solicitor will most want to focus while it is still in draft form are:

- Does it contain the basic minimum of information about the **expert and his credentials** for writing the report, the dispute to which it relates and the party on whose behalf it has been prepared?
- Does it state accurately the **substance of all instructions** received by the expert, whether written or oral, on the basis of which the report has been written?
- Does it **fulfil the brief** given?

Report must include detail on literature, background, tests, facts, inferences and contradictions

Where relevant, the report should also:

- give details of the **technical literature** or any other material on which the expert has relied
- provide all necessary **background information** for an understanding of the investigations undertaken or the methodology used
- state **who conducted the tests** and experiments (if any) the expert has used for the report and their qualifications for carrying them out
- set out the **facts ascertained** and the **inferences drawn** from them, with convincing reasoning for doing so
- analyse, and if possible account for, any **contradictions** that may have emerged in the

course of fact gathering or were revealed in documents disclosed by the other side.

In any event, the solicitor will wish to ensure that:

- the report **summarises the expert's findings**
- the report **provides a clear statement of opinion** as to what happened and/or why it happened
- all expressions of opinion are confined to matters **within the expert's competence**.

Report must summarise findings and give opinion

If any question should have arisen as to whether what was done conformed to normal practice, the report should identify any relevant recognised body of opinion regarding normal practice which differs from that of the expert, and give the expert's reasons for his opinion.

Report must identify differing bodies of opinion

Finally, the solicitor will wish to check that the report satisfies two specific requirements of the practice direction concerning experts and assessors, namely that it:

Report must conclude with statement of truth

- **concludes with a statement** to the effect that the expert understands his duty to the court and has complied with that duty, and
- **is verified by a 'statement of truth'** in the form laid down in the Practice Direction.[8]

Privilege

In the current context, privilege is a legal concept. A golden rule for any expert should be that legal issues are a matter for lawyers, not experts. Accordingly, experts could simply ignore whether privilege does, or does not, exist for a particular document. However, an expert will be likely to enjoy better

---

[8] For the text of the Practice Direction, see *Appendix 2: CPR Part 35 Practice Direction* on page 190.

relationships with instructing lawyers if a clear stance on the treatment of documents (including verbal briefings) is established at the outset.

Expert instructions

Woolf wanted to ensure unsupportive material and opinion heard

In the Interim Report on his inquiry, Lord Woolf argued that once the decision is taken to instruct an expert to prepare a report for use in court, *all* communications between the instructing party and its expert should be made available to the party's opponents. The intention behind this radical proposal was **to prevent the suppression of factual material or expert opinion that did not support the case**.

By the time he wrote his Final Report, however, Lord Woolf had come to accept that a waiver of privilege on all communications with experts was not the best way forward. But he still regarded it as essential that under the new system – and especially in cases (e.g. fast track) where expert evidence would be limited to written reports – it was essential for the parties and the judge to know:

- the **basis on which the experts were providing the report**
- the **factual information supplied to them** by their instructing solicitors.

Accordingly, Lord Woolf recommended that an expert report should not be admissible unless there was annexed to it all the written instructions the expert had received, together with a note of any oral instructions given.

Report must state substance of all material instructions

In the event, this recommendation was further watered down by the committee drafting the new CPR. All that Rule 35.10(3) specifies is that an expert's report '*must state the substance of all material instructions, whether written or oral, on the basis of which the report was written'.*

Furthermore, the succeeding paragraph makes clear that, although instructions are not privileged against disclosure, a court will not order the disclosure of any specific document, nor permit cross-examination on it, *'unless it is satisfied that there are reasonable grounds to consider the statement of instructions given under paragraph (3) to be inaccurate or incomplete.'*

Court will not probe instructions without reasonable grounds

Rule 35.10 also states that an expert report must comply with the requirements set out in the practice direction on experts and assessors. This provides a useful gloss on what is meant by 'the substance of material instructions'.

Guidance on 'substance of material instructions'

The practice direction stipulates that the statement of instructions set out in an expert report *'should summarise the facts and instructions given to the expert that are material to the opinions expressed in the report or upon which those opinions are based.'* It elsewhere requires that an expert report must give details of any literature or other material the expert has relied on in making the report.

Summarise facts and instructions material to opinion

Consider the question, then: 'Must I list in my report all the documents I have seen?' These two provisions would suggest the answer: 'Only if they provided you with information unavailable elsewhere or influenced in any way the opinion you expressed.'

Should experts list all documents seen?

However, matters may not be quite so straightforward if the document you saw was, for example, another professional's opinion, as happened in the case of *Clough -v- Tameside and Glossop Health Authority.*[9]

---

[9] *Clough -v- Tameside & Glossop Health Authority* [1998] 2 *AER* 971.

Substance of instructions

In *Clough* the claimant was suing the defendant for negligence. The defendant served an expert report produced by Dr Hay. The latter referred to the fact that he had been supplied with a further report by Dr Pandy for consideration. The claimant wanted to see Dr Pandy's report. The defendant resisted on the basis that Dr Pandy's report been brought into existence for the purpose of the litigation and was therefore privileged. That privilege had not been waived by a mere reference to it by Dr Hay in his report. The defendant also argued that the Pandy report was irrelevant since it had played no part in helping Dr Hay to arrive at his conclusions.

The judge in the case reviewed a number of authorities and held that there had been waiver or that she should exercise her discretion to override the privilege. She ordered production.

Lawyers must take extreme care to avoid unintended disclosure

Following the court's decision in this case it was necessary for lawyers to exercise extreme caution when providing an expert with instructions and materials. Otherwise there was a real danger that there would be an unintended loss of privilege that would render such instructions or documents disclosable.

The Court of Appeal gave further consideration to this question in *Lucas -v- Barking, Havering & Redbridge Hospital NHS Trust*.[10] In its decision, the Court of Appeal reaffirmed that the obligation of an expert is to 'state the substance of all material instructions, whether written or oral, on the basis of which the report was written' [CPR 35.10(3)]. **One should note that there is an important distinction between 'substance' and 'material'.** The relevant

---

[10] *Lucas -v- Barking, Havering & Redbridge Hospital NHS Trust* [2003] *EWCA Civ* 1102.

Practice Direction provides that the report must contain 'a statement setting out the substance of all facts and instructions given to the expert that are material to the opinions expressed in the report or upon which those opinions are based' [CPR 35 PD2.2(3)].

Deployment required to waive privilege

The Court of Appeal took the view that the appeal raised a fundamental question as to what effect the CPR were intended to have on the broader question of privilege.

In the case of *Bourns Inc -v- Raychem Corp & Another*[11] it had been established, by reference to *Clough*, that service of a witness statement, be it a statement from an expert or a witness of fact, waives privilege in that statement. Mere reference to a document does not waive privilege – there must, at least, be reference to the contents and reliance thereon. Simply stated, there must have been 'deployment' of the document for privilege to be waived.

Document must be deployed for privilege to be waived

Under CPR 35.10(3) there is a compulsion on experts to set out their material instructions. This contrasts with the discretion a party will otherwise have in choosing to refer to a document in a statement of claim or witness statement that might otherwise be privileged. CPR 35.10(3) compels disclosure of what would otherwise be privileged material. Indeed, by reference to the fact that experts need only refer to material instructions, it strongly implies that the documents have been material to the expert's consideration of the matter and have, therefore, been 'deployed' as opposed to simply 'noted'.

---

[11] *Bourns Inc -v- Raychem Corp & Another* [1999] 3 *AER* 154.

Protection remains for some documents

The Court of Appeal concluded that the intention behind the CPR 35.10(4) barrier to automatic disclosure must have been to encourage the expert to comply with the duty to set out the substance of all material instructions. Furthermore, because of the compulsory nature of this duty, it must be intended to afford some protection in relation to documents that would otherwise become disclosable and in respect of which there had been no other indication that privilege had been waived.

'Defining 'instructions'

Broad definition of 'instructions' preferred

Waller LJ, in *Lucas*, leaned towards the view that, in so far as material supplied to expert witnesses is concerned, a wide construction of the word 'instructions' was to be preferred. This would include:

- all information supplied by the party, and
- all information the instructing solicitor might place before the expert to obtain advice.

Accordingly, it was held that material supplied by an instructing party to an expert witness as the basis on which the expert was being asked to advise should be considered part of the instructions and thus be subject to CPR 35.10(4).

'Material' does not necessarily mean 'all'

There would, of course, be an obvious answer to be made in opposition to any claim to protection under CPR 35.10(4). The requesting party could continue to say that the documents were disclosable because the expert had not stated the substance of all material instructions.

No requirement to set out all information or material provided, just the material instructions

The Court of Appeal dealt with this question by clarifying the meaning of CPR 35.10(3). It concluded that there is no requirement to set out all the information provided in the statement or all the material supplied to the expert. The only obligation on the expert is to **set out material instructions**. ('Material' means information considered by the expert to have been relevant to the opinion formed.) The protection applies to any particular document or any particular question over any area. This is because disclosure of any part of privileged material will otherwise imply waiver of privilege once deployed.

Note of caution

The decision of the Court of Appeal is regarded by some as a retrogressive step. Criticism centres on the fact that an expert witness might have access to materials upon which some reliance was placed but which are not accessible to another party or their expert.

Take, for example, a case where the expert has been provided with a draft pleading or a draft witness statement which differs in substance from that eventually put before the court at trial. What mechanisms are in place to ensure that this is brought to the attention of the court and that the issues are dealt with justly?

The *Lucas* decision leaves many questions unanswered. It should, therefore, be treated with caution. A solicitor who supplies an expert with documents intended to be privileged still risks the unintended loss of this privilege if the expert fails to set out the material instructions in such a way as to satisfy CPR 35.10(3).

Solicitor risks unintended loss of privilege if expert fails to satisfy CPR 35.10(3)

It seems inevitable that this difficult area will be the subject of further appeals. In the meantime, expert witnesses should ensure that they comply with the rules governing the preparation of their reports. If in doubt, they should seek guidance. In addition, it remains true that instructing solicitors should be extremely wary about sending an expert any materials they do not wish the opposing side(s) to see.

Assume no privilege will be claimed

Assume instructions contain no privileged information

The CPR and the CJC *Experts Protocol* require an expert to be transparent in his formulation of the mandatory statement of the substance of all material instructions. Therefore an expert should assume that his instructions do not contain any information for which privilege would be claimed.

3
The Report

In the context of litigation it is important to distinguish between two kinds of expert report:

* those commissioned solely for the **advice** of an instructing solicitor or lay client, and
* those required for the **purpose of court proceedings**.

While it is with the latter that this chapter is concerned, much of what follows will be relevant to both kinds of report. The legal requirements, though, apply only to those intended for use in court.

In general, expert witnesses are immune from suit in respect of reports they prepare for court purposes, but this is not the case with those they write to *advise* their clients. With such reports, they are as liable in negligence for the opinions they express as they would be for reports written for any other professional purpose.

Careful!
Which sort of report are you being asked to write? Issues of immunity and liability arise.

Significance of expert reports

The production of a report is central to the role of an expert witness. This is so whether or not the case goes to trial. Indeed, 95% of civil cases never reach court: they are either settled beforehand or abandoned altogether. Reports commissioned from experts can play just as crucial a role in securing

Reports are regularly used to negotiate a settlement

such outcomes as they can in cases that get to court.

Equally high standards apply to preparing reports as to giving oral evidence in court

The majority of civil cases will not result in a court appearance. But acceptance of instructions as an expert witness, particularly in connection with higher value or more complex claims, always carries with it the possibility of being called to the witness box. In such circumstances the expert's examination-in-chief, cross-examination and re-examination would be based on the report addressed previously to the court. It follows that the same standards are required of experts for the reports they write as for any evidence they may give from the witness box. The most succinct definition of this requirement that we have come across is that **expert witnesses need to be truthful as to fact, thorough in technical reasoning, honest as to opinion and complete in coverage of relevant matters.**[1]

Purpose of expert reports

A report must inform the court, with opinion linked to fact

The primary goal of a report written for court purposes is to inform, not to win the case – the latter is the lawyer's job. Typically, an expert report will provide:

- a **comprehensive account** of those matters the expert was instructed to investigate
- a **rigorous analysis** of this information, and
- a **clear conclusion** summarising the issues and giving the **expert's opinion** on them.

As explained in Chapter 1, the essential characteristic of expert evidence is that it is *opinion* evidence. In the context of litigation, the whole point of commissioning an expert report is to get the expert to deliver that opinion with as much

---

[1] *Surveyors Acting as Expert Witnesses* [1997] RICS, London, UK.

supporting detail and analysis as is necessary to convince those reading the report that it is well founded.

Scope

It is important to note, too, that the court will expect the report to give the expert's opinion **in its entirety**. Just as the parties to a dispute have a duty to disclose *all* relevant documents in their possession or control [CPR 31.6(b)(i)], including any that may adversely affect their case or support that of another party, so too must experts endeavour to report on **all matters within their expertise** concerning the issues on which they have been instructed. This includes findings that may prove detrimental to their instructing party's case or favour that of the opponents.

A report must contain the expert's opinion in its entirety

Detrimental findings must also be included

The CPR lay down that it is the duty of expert witnesses to help the court on all matters within their expertise, and that this duty overrides any obligation the experts may have to those paying them. As if to reinforce this statement, the associated Practice Direction requires that experts address their reports to the court and not to the parties who instructed them. In such circumstances it would be wholly wrong for an expert to submit a report to the court that omitted potentially damaging opinions, or to communicate them solely to his instructing solicitor.

Reports are addressed to the court, not to the parties – no hired guns here!

It would be no less wrong, of course, for the solicitor to ask the expert to amend, expand or otherwise alter the report in a way that distorts the expert's opinion. On the other hand, it **is** in order for the solicitor to suggest to the expert that the report be amended or expanded in the interests of accuracy and consistency, to improve its clarity or to ensure its completeness.

Reports can be amended to improve clarity, consistency and accuracy – but NOT to change opinion

Legal requirements

Duties of an expert witness summarised by Cresswell and Toulmin (see page 212)

There are few statutory requirements regarding expert evidence, but plenty of case law. The salient features were distilled by Mr Justice Cresswell in his judgment in the *Ikarian Reefer* case and updated by Judge John Toulmin CMG QC in *Anglo Group plc -v- Winther Brown & Co Ltd and BML (Office Computers) Ltd.*[2]

The 'Cresswell principles' have come to be accepted as providing the classic statement of the duties and responsibilities of expert witnesses. They have been endorsed by the Court of Appeal and commended by Lord Woolf in his Inquiry into the civil justice system in England and Wales. This is not to say, though, that they are entirely unambiguous or, for that matter, entirely reasonable – as Anthony Speaight QC demonstrates in a commentary on them available in *Appendix 4: Cresswell and Toulmin* starting on page 212.

Procedural issues

A report written in contemplation of litigation is privileged

An expert report produced in the course of litigation is subject to legal privilege[3]. Should the commissioning party not like the conclusions its expert has reached and decides against relying upon them, that party need not disclose the report to the other side. Providing the court agrees, the party still has the option, should it wish, to commission a fresh report from another expert.

There's no property in an expert

But there is no property in an expert. Indeed, if a party's opponents should get wind that the expert

---

[2] *Anglo Group plc -v- Winther Brown & Co Ltd and BML (Office Computers) Ltd* [2000] *EWHC Technology* 127.

[3] Except, that is, for medical reports obtained in connection with Children Act proceedings. Family Procedure (Adoption) Rules 2005, rule 163(4).

has turned in an adverse report, they are entirely within their rights to call that expert themselves. Moreover, because the court is entitled to have all the relevant evidence drawn to its attention, it would be quite wrong for the solicitor who originally instructed the expert to try to prevent that expert giving evidence for the other side.

In the great majority of cases, of course, a party to a dispute will wish to make use of the reports it has commissioned. To do so it will need first of all to disclose them to the other party or parties. This may be done:

- **by agreement between the parties**, often in the expectation that the evidence itself will be agreed and can form the basis for a negotiated settlement, or
- **by order of the court** at the allocation stage of the proceedings. If disclosure is ordered, the court will normally insist on the simultaneous exchange of reports by a specified date.

Exchange will usually be arranged via the parties's lawyers, and an expert witness should always seek instructions before agreeing to make an exchange direct with the expert for the other side.

Experts should never disclose reports without checking with the instructing lawyer

The main purpose of the rules governing the exchange of expert reports is:

- to **encourage prior agreement on issues of fact**, with a consequential saving in the court's time
- to **prevent one side from 'ambushing' the other** in court
- to **ensure that both sides have the same opportunity to prepare** their cases as thoroughly as possible.

65

Reports cannot be re-used without permission of the expert and that of the original client

It is worth noting here that when expert reports are exchanged in pursuance of court rules, the parties to whom they are thereby disclosed are debarred from making any collateral use of them, e.g. in other litigation, whether or not related to the case for which they have been exchanged. (See *Re-use of expert reports* on page 85.) The obligation not to make collateral use is one owed to the court under whose aegis the exchange was effected. Should an expert find that it has happened, the matter should be brought to the attention of the court.

Civil Procedure Rules

Requirements set out in Part 35, associated Practice Direction and Pre-action Protocols

The formal requirements regarding expert reports are set out in Part 35 of the CPR (see *Appendix 1: CPR Part 35*), in the associated Practice Direction on experts and assessors (see *Appendix 2: CPR Part 35 Practice Direction*) and, where applicable, in pre-action protocols.[4] They give effect to many, but not all, of the recommendations on expert evidence made by Lord Woolf in the Final Report of his inquiry.

As is well known, the basic reform proposed by Lord Woolf was that in future it should be the court, not the litigants, that directs the conduct and pace of litigation. By entrusting the management of cases to the judiciary, he envisaged that:

- litigation could be made **less adversarial**
- its **timescale shortened** and
- its **cost much reduced**.

As a result, litigation ought to become more affordable, the decision more predictable and the

---

[4] For the full text of Part 35 of the CPR and of the related Practice Direction on experts and assessors, see Appendix 1: CPR Part 35 and Appendix 2: CPR Part 35 Practice Direction.

outcome more proportionate to the value and complexity of the claim.

In furtherance of these aims, Lord Woolf made a number of recommendations concerning expert evidence, of which those affecting expert reports may be summarised as follows:

Woolf reforms to promote affordability, predictability and proportionality

- The calling of expert evidence should be under the **complete control of the court**.

- **Single joint experts** should be used wherever possible, and if need be the court should have the power to appoint that expert.

- The **primary responsibility of experts is to the court**, and it is to the court that their reports should be addressed.

- Experts must annex to their reports all the **written instructions** they received, including letters subsequent upon the original instructions, and a note of any oral instruction.

- A party should have the **right to put written questions** to the other party's expert about his report.

- Each report should end with a **declaration** that it includes everything the expert regards as relevant to the opinion expressed and should draw attention to any matter that would affect the validity of that opinion.

Woolf's key recommendations concerning expert evidence

These concerns were duly reflected in the draft CPR published at the same time as Lord Woolf's report. But several of them were watered down over the 18 months it took to finalise the Rules. So, for example, the appointment of experts by the court is now to be seen as the option of last resort.

Court-appointed experts are a last resort

CPR resources

Appendix 1:
CPR Part 35

Appendix 2:
Part 35 PD

The CPR and Practice Directions undergo periodic review. A copy of Part 35 of the CPR current at the time of publishing can be viewed in *Appendix 1: CPR Part 35* and its associated Practice Direction in *Appendix 2: CPR Part 35 Practice Direction*.

CJC Experts Protocol

Appendix 3:
CJC Experts
Protocol

The CJC *Experts Protocol* has been inculcated into the CPR by referral from the Part 35 Practice Direction. See *Appendix 3: Annotated CJC Experts Protocol* for full details and a discussion.

Structure and content

Reports must balance detail and readability

The requirements of litigation dictate the content, structure, style and layout of reports written for use in court proceedings. As a result, the form such reports take will often be quite unlike that of others an expert might write in the course of his professional work. For one thing, the arrangement of the report must reflect the need to convince its readers that the author is qualified to express the opinions offered and to reach the conclusions made; for another, it has to be pitched at the level of understanding of an intelligent reader who has little or no knowledge of the report's subject matter.

Although there are now some formal requirements concerning expert reports (see *Appendices 1–3*), it is simply not feasible to lay down hard and fast rules as to their content: the cases for which they may be required are too diverse for that. For example, a construction engineer's report on the collapse of a building is likely to be much more extensive than one an orthopaedic surgeon might write on a leg injury. Conversely, a doctor's report in a medical negligence case will probably require much more detailed consideration of the patient's case notes than an engineer's report would of a car's service history. In short, the nature of the case and of the issues the expert has been instructed to investigate will largely determine the content of the report. What matters far more is that in writing it the expert:

- addresses the real issues presented by the case
- provides the information in a logical way
- reaches a clear conclusion, and
- does not stray beyond the limits of professional competence.

Reports must be the independent product of the expert

It is to be hoped, though, that solicitors do not take what follows to be either mandatory or all-embracing, still less that it should dictate the arrangement of the various sections of a report, for that would make them even more indigestible that they too often are. If a report is to be, in the words of Mr Justice Cresswell, the 'independent product of the expert', it must allow the individuality of the expert to show through.

Law Society guidance

That said, it is useful to have some general guidance on what an expert report should include, and that offered by the Law Society in its 'Code of Practice: Expert Witnesses engaged by Solicitors' provides a useful starting point. In essence it reads:

'The report should cover:

(a) basic information such as names and dates

(b) the source of the instructions and the purpose of the report

(c) the history of the matter

(d) the methodology used in the investigation

(e) the documents referred to in the preparation of the report and/or any evidence upon which the report is based

(f) facts ascertained

(g) inferences drawn from the facts, with reasoning

(h) the conclusions, cross-referenced to the text, and

(i) the expert's qualifications and experience.'

CPR Part 35

Certain formal requirements for expert reports are specified in Part 35 of the CPR (see *Appendix 1: CPR Part 35*) and its associated Practice Direction.

Part 35 PD: specific directions as to form and content of report

The Practice Direction on Experts and Assessors (see *Appendix 2: CPR Part 35 Practice Direction*) is altogether more specific as to the form and content required of reports for use in court proceedings. Although it involves some repetition, the relevant section is worth reproducing here in full. It reads as follows:

'2.1 An expert's report should be addressed to the court and not to the party from whom the expert has received his instructions.

2.2 An expert's report must:

(1) give details of the expert's qualifications;

(2) give details of any literature or other material which the expert has relied on in making the report;

(3) contain a statement setting out the substance of all facts and instructions given to the expert which are material to the opinions expressed in the report or upon which those opinions are based;

(4) make clear which of the facts stated in the report are within the expert's own knowledge;

(5) say who carried out any examination, measurement, test or experiment which the expert has used for the report, give the qualifications of that person, and say whether or not the test or experiment has been carried out under the expert's supervision;

(6) where there is a range of opinion on the matters dealt with in the report –

(a) summarise the range of opinion, and

(b) give reasons for his own opinion;

(7) contain a summary of the conclusions reached;

(8) if the expert is not able to give his opinion without qualification, state the qualification; and

(9) contain a statement that the expert understands his duty to the court, and has complied and will continue to comply with that duty.

2.3 An expert's report must be verified by a statement of truth as well as containing the statements required in paragraph 2.2(8) and (9) above.

2.4 The form of the statement of truth is as follows:

"I confirm that insofar as the facts stated in my report are within my own knowledge I have made clear which they are and I believe them to be true, and that the opinions I have expressed represent my true and complete professional opinion."

2.5 Attention is drawn to rule 32.14 which sets out the consequences of verifying a document containing a false statement without an honest belief in its truth.'

(For information about statements of truth see Part 22 and the supplementary practice direction.)

While several of these requirements are taken straight from Part 35 of the Rules, it is worth noting that some are quite new. Of particular importance are the stipulations that experts must:

- summarise any **range of opinion** that may exist about matters dealt with in their reports
- verify the reports with a mandatory **statement of truth**.

CJC Experts Protocol

Protocol extends guidance

The CJC *Experts Protocol* dedicates an entire section to the content of the expert report (see *Experts Protocol 13: Contents of Experts' Reports* on page 202). It starts by iterating CPR Part 35 and its associated Practice Direction, before dealing with a number of specific items.

Qualifications

In most cases a simple list of an expert's academic, professional or job-related qualifications will suffice. In more complex cases, requiring the use of highly specialised expertise, an expert should include information on specific training and/or experience that supports the claim of enhanced expertise.

Tests and reliance on the work of others

The methodology of any tests carried out should be included in an expert report. If such tests – or, indeed, any other aspect of the expert report – are based on the work of others, those individuals should be identified and their qualifications given. If any of this material has not been independently verified by the expert, that should be noted clearly in the report.

Work of others must be acknowledged and identified

Facts

Experts should always keep facts and opinions apart. When expressing an opinion, the expert should identify which facts (assumed or otherwise) underpin it.

Separate fact and opinion

If any of the facts are disputed, the expert should give an opinion on each separate hypothesis without expressing which opinion is favoured – unless, on the basis of expert knowledge, one set of facts is found to be improbable.

Disputed facts need special attention

Range of opinion

If the mandatory summary of the range of opinion is based on published sources, experts should explain those sources and, where appropriate, state the qualifications of the originator(s) of the opinions from which they differ, particularly if such opinions represent a well-established school of thought.

Range of opinion must be presented and justified

Where there is no available source for the range of opinion, experts may need to express opinions on what they believe to be the range which other experts would arrive at if asked. In those circumstances, experts should make it clear that the range they summarise is based on their own judgment and explain the basis of that judgment.

Ideal structure

Cross-referencing essential for accessibility

Clearly, expert reports need to be accessible to those for whom they are prepared. They should follow a logical sequence, bearing in mind the uses to which they may be put. Furthermore, if they are more than a few pages long, it is important that they are cross-referenced in a manner that makes it easy to move from fact to opinion, and back again, and to call up supporting documentation.

Keep opinion until the end, rather than scattering it throughout

The precise structure of an expert report will depend, like its content, on the complexity of the matter under investigation. At the very least, though, it should have a beginning (introduction and background), a middle (facts and analysis) and an end (opinion or conclusion), with further subdivisions as appropriate and appendices bringing up the rear. Most important of all, opinion should always be seen to follow the facts. Keep opinion until the end, rather than presenting it piecemeal throughout the report.

Introduction

Identify author, dispute and commissioning party

Because each report has to be complete in itself, an introduction is needed to identify its author, the dispute to which the report relates and the party on whose behalf it is prepared. It should also set out the brief received, demonstrate the expert's fitness to carry out the instructions, and specify the principal sources of information on which the expert has relied.

It is in the introduction that the expert needs to show that the matter on which opinion is being sought lies within his field of expertise. Here, too, the expert should identify any colleagues who may have assisted in the investigations, together with their qualifications for doing so, and those others on whose opinions the expert will be relying. The introduction is also the appropriate place for an expert to indicate any actual or potential conflict of interest that may have come to light since instructions to write the report were accepted (see page 22).

Define substance of instructions and suitability of expertise for case

Highlight conflicts of interest, if any

From CPR 35.10 it is apparent that while experts are not now expected to reproduce in their entirety the instructions they receive, they could still come a cropper if they were tempted, for whatever reason, to skimp the task of stating their 'substance'. Such a failure could well open them to some tough questioning along the lines of 'What were you told about this case before you were formally instructed?', 'How many draft stages has your report been through?' and 'What changes were you asked to make to your report?' Clearly, some care is called for to ensure this does not happen. Fortunately the Practice Direction (see *Appendix 2: CPR Part 35 Practice Direction*) provides rather more guidance as to what the Rules mean by 'substance'. (For a discussion on this topic see page 56.)

Experts must state the 'substance' of their instructions

Background

Here the scene is set for much of what follows. In a medical negligence case, say, it might take the form of a brief history of the patient's illness prior to receiving the treatment in dispute. In a construction case, it might detail the location, construction history

Scene setting with non-controversial facts and history

and dimensions of the building concerned. The expert may also find it convenient to list at this point the technical issues to be addressed in the main body of the report that follows. All the material included in this section should be entirely factual and non-controversial.

Facts of the case

State agreed facts, identify documents and statements, state assumptions

Now we get to the substance of the report, though just how extensive the section will be depends on the number and complexity of the issues to be examined. The facts of the matter in dispute need to be set out fully and, once again, in a completely non-controversial way. All the documents and statements referred to should be identified clearly. If the expert has been told to assume certain facts, then these should be distinguished from those observed by the expert, e.g. when examining the patient or visiting the scene of an accident. This section should also include a description of any tests or experiments the expert carried out in the course of the investigation, or that others conducted on his behalf, with the results.

Describe tests and experiments, and give factual results – no opinion

Analysis

The analytical part of the expert report should include:

- the **unravelling of any contradictions** that may have emerged in the course of fact gathering, and
- the **interpretation of the results** of any investigations or experiments that may have been undertaken to account for what occurred.

It is here that the expert's specialist knowledge and experience are brought into play, and where the

76

expert may draw on the opinions of others or cite recognised statements of professional practice.

The trap to be avoided at all costs is that of minimising or glossing over findings that may be detrimental to the client. It is far better to air them in the report than to have them dragged out in cross-examination. It could be, too, that reporting such findings may provide just the impetus needed to persuade the parties to negotiate a settlement.

Don't minimise the significance of detrimental findings

Turning to the reporting of experimental evidence, there has been some difference of opinion among judges as to whether experts need to include in, or append to, their reports *all* their results, including those of experiments that led nowhere or proved irrelevant.[5] On the one hand, there are those who maintain that failure to report findings that do not support the opinion being advanced is tantamount to misleading the court. Other judges fear that to require experts to include everything, when there may be perfectly good and sensible reasons for not doing so, would needlessly increase the length and cost of expert reports.

How should experimental evidence be included?

The CPR are silent on this issue, as is the Practice Direction on Experts and Assessors. However, other requirements relating to tests or experiments are stated to apply only to those *the expert has used for the report*. It might be deduced from this that experiments, etc., not used need not be reported. To argue thus can be dangerous, though, because the overriding objective of the CPR is **to enable the court to deal with cases justly**, and judges are required to interpret them in that light. In due course too, means may be found for reinstating a requirement dropped by the Rules Committee at the

Guidance unclear, but remember the overriding objective

---

[5] See, for example, Mr Justice Laddie's judgment in *Electrolux Northern Ltd -v- Black & Decker Ltd* [1996] *FSR* 595.

final stage of revision, namely that experts should draw the attention of the court to any matter that would affect the validity of the opinions expressed.

Conclusions

In *Conclusions* the expert should:

- **summarise** what the investigations yielded on each of the issues considered and
- **set out the expert opinion** as to what happened, why it happened or whether what was done conformed to normal practice.

End reports with a statement of truth

The report should finish with the mandatory statement of truth, the wording of which is:

> *'I confirm that insofar as the facts stated in my report are within my own knowledge I have made clear which they are and I believe them to be true, and that the opinions I have expressed represent my true and complete professional opinion.'*

The original and all copies of the report should be dated and signed by the expert.

Appendices

Use appendices to store technical data, codes of practice, calculations, etc.

Appendices should be used wherever detail threatens to obscure the main thrust of the report or confuse the reader. They could include with advantage:

- a **list of the published material** referred to in the report
- if the report relies on many documents, these **documents can be listed** in the appendix, rather than in the body of the report
- all **experimental readings and calculations** referred to in the main part of the report

- copies of relevant **technical data**
- extracts from **codes of practice**, etc., cited in the report
- in complex cases, a **chronology of events**
- **a glossary** of technical terms.

Style

There is no such thing as a standard style for reports, and experts should be wary of adopting one that is foreign to them. Providing certain fundamentals are observed, experts should use the style with which they are most comfortable.

The fundamentals are accuracy in spelling, consistency in punctuation and, above all, clarity of expression. Keep sentences short, use the active voice as far as possible and, above all, avoid professional jargon. If it should prove absolutely necessary to use technical words or phrases, provide definitions of them, but relegate these to a glossary rather than risk appearing to explain things the readers of the report already know.

Accurate spelling, consistent punctuation, clarity; avoid jargon, use a glossary

Layout

All reports should be typed on A4 paper and on one side of the sheet only. The text should be well spaced, with short paragraphs, each one of which is restricted to one topic. Wide margins should be left to allow space for readers's notes and comments. As an aid to their location, sections, paragraphs and sub-paragraphs should all be numbered, and the same numbering system adopted throughout.

One-sided A4, well spaced text, wide margins, short numbered paragraphs

The front cover of the report should state:

Front cover requirements

- the title of the action
- the name of the party for whom it has been prepared

- the aspects of the matter the report addresses
- the author's name, qualifications and contact details, and
- the date of the report's completion.

Final page requirements

All subsequent pages must be numbered, and the final page signed and dated by the author. In the case of reports prepared for use in court, this page is also the one on which any formal statements required by the court should appear.

If the report should be exceptionally long, it may be advisable to insert a contents page ahead of the introduction, and an executive summary of the writer's conclusions immediately after it. This last is optional, however, and experts need not be too concerned if counsel should ask for it to be removed while their reports are still in draft.

Sanctions and problems

Wasted costs orders are possible – even against the expert

Expert evidence thrown out

It is important to remember that the court has the power to penalise any party whose expert infringes the CPR and Practice Direction, and it can do so in a number of ways. At one end of the scale it may make an adverse costs order (e.g. by disallowing recovery of the expert's fees and expenses from the opposing party), while at the other extreme it could debar the instructing party from making any use of the expert's evidence.

Another point experts need to bear in mind is that under the system of case management introduced by the CPR, the great majority of cases that go to trial will be assigned to the 'fast track'. In such cases it will be rare that experts will be required to give their evidence in court. On the other hand, judges will get to see the reports they write well before cases come to trial. It follows that, if a report should be found wanting in any respect, it may well dictate the outcome of a case on the small claims and fast tracks. For a case on the multi-track, though, it would be likely to place the expert at a distinct disadvantage in the witness box.

Uncomfortable cross-examination

Lastly, the tight timetabling the Rules prescribe for the conduct of fast-track cases means that an expert who has been instructed on behalf of just one of the parties will have fewer than 10 weeks in which:

Tight timetabling adds pressure

- to digest any new information disclosed by the other parties
- to prepare a draft report for submission to his instructing solicitor, and
- to prepare the final version of the report for exchange with the other side.

This merely adds to the pressure on litigants to make joint appointments of single experts wherever possible.

Changes to the report

An instructing solicitor can ask for an expert's report to be amended if:

Experts should be prepared to amend reports to improve clarity

- it does not conform to CPR requirements
- the facts it is based upon are wrong
- relevant material is not included
- the presentation of the opinion is not as clear as it might be.

The expert should not object to the solicitor probing the *meaning* of what has been written. It is, after all, in everyone's interest that the evidence should be clear.

If new facts come to light after the report has been written, but before it has been disclosed, it is quite normal to modify the report. If, however, the report has been disclosed, it is better to write a supplementary report. Supplementary reports usually have to be authorised by the court before they can be relied upon.

A good approach when preparing a supplementary report (recommended by Edge Ellison, Solicitors) is to take each issue in turn in the following way:

> *'Heading (the issue being addressed)*
>
> *In my main report I said that [summarise briefly what you said in the main report by reference to numbered paragraphs if appropriate].*
>
> *The defence (or other document in which the issue in question is raised) raised the following issue: [summarise briefly the new issue raised]*
>
> *[Summarise the position taking that issue into account].*
>
> *I now put forward the following opinion:*
>
> *[...] (expanding on paragraphs [ ] to [ ] of my main report; and/or*
>
> *[...] (in place of paragraphs [ ] to [ ] of my main report); and/or*
>
> *[...] (additional material).*
>
> *[Summarise the overall position on the new issue.]'*

Experts should never amend opinion unless a fault in reasoning is demonstrated

What the solicitor may not do, and the expert should *never* agree to do, is to require that the opinion expressed in the report be altered. The only exception is when a fault in reasoning can be demonstrated.[6] In any event, a solicitor may not alter, or allow others to alter, the text of an expert's report in any particular without the expert's permission. Neither may the solicitor use the report, nor allow others to do so, for any purpose other than litigation in the matter on which the expert was originally instructed.

Privilege

As far as expert witnesses are concerned, the issues of privilege and disclosure relate mostly, although not entirely, to expert reports. Indeed, in many cases such issues will not arise at all. With personal injury claims, for instance, it often happens that an expert report is served on the defendant with the statement of claim, and any privilege attaching to it is thereby waived at that early stage in the proceedings. This is not to say, though, that the expert's involvement with the report is now at an end. It could be that subsequent disclosure of the defendant's evidence will necessitate a rethink on the expert's part. If that should lead to any modification of the opinions expressed in the original report, the expert will need to inform the claimant's solicitor straightaway.

In personal injury claims, the norm is disclosure of report at the outset with statement of claim

In circumstances where an expert's report has *not* been served on the other party at the outset of the case, the timing of its subsequent disclosure will be determined by the court at the allocation stage, i.e. when the case is assigned to one of the three 'tracks' and the date of the hearing set.

When not served at outset, timing of report disclosure set at allocation stage

- For a case on the **small claims** track the court would normally require all documents, including expert reports, to be served at least 14 days before the hearing.

Small claims: disclosure at least 14 days before hearing

---

[6] CJC *Experts Protocol* 15, see page 204.

Fast track: disclosure within 14 weeks of allocation date

- If it is on the **fast track**, standard directions would require reports to be exchanged no later than 14 weeks from the date of allocation to the track. Since the aim is that fast-track cases should be brought to trial within 30 weeks of allocation, this means that parties have approximately 4 months in which to consider the reports of their opponent's experts, put written questions about them, prepare supplementary reports where needed, reassess their own chances of success at trial and, if it is thought desirable, seek a negotiated settlement. Clearly, the fast track is intended to live up to its name!

Multi-track: no predetermined constraints but court direction

- With cases on the **multi-track**, there are no predetermined constraints of this kind, and the directions the court gives for the exchange of expert reports will take account of the complexity of the claim and, to some extent, the needs of the parties. Once the date has been set, though, the court will expect it to be kept and can penalise parties that miss the deadline.

Simultaneous exchange the norm, but staged disclosure an option

Experts should note that while simultaneous exchange of reports is the norm, the court may, if it thinks fit, order disclosure by stages, allowing one party the opportunity to consider the report from its opponent's expert before disclosing that of its own.

Are draft reports privileged?

Experts should note, too, that it is only *final* reports that are exchanged, i.e. those on which the parties intend to rely and on which, in multi-track cases, the experts themselves may be cross-examined in court. This poses the question whether privilege continues to attach to *draft* reports once final reports have been exchanged. Some commentators hold that after exchange privilege in the drafts is also waived. But this would not appear to have been Lord Woolf's

intention when framing the new procedures. In the
Final Report of his inquiry he wrote:

> *'The point has been made that experts must
> be free to submit drafts to clients and their
> legal advisers, so that factual misconceptions
> can be corrected. A further objection is that a
> great deal of time could be wasted if all these
> documents were disclosable, because the
> opposing party would have to comb through
> the various versions of a report to identify any
> changes, the reasons for which would not
> always be clear in any event... I accept, in the
> light of these arguments, that it would not be
> realistic to make draft experts' reports
> disclosable.'*

**Woolf intended
drafts to remain
privileged**

Nonetheless, the possibility remains that a party
might apply for specific disclosure of a draft report in
circumstances where it has reason to suspect that
the lawyers for the other side have done a good deal
more than correct 'factual misconceptions' in their
expert's draft. For the expert to agree to make
changes of a more fundamental nature than that
might well compromise the duty of independence
owed the court.

**But disclosure
could be sought if
lawyers thought
to have influenced
opinion**

Re-use of expert reports

Experts occasionally find that a report they prepared
for one case has been (or is about to be) re-used in
satellite litigation, or even for a completely different
purpose. Such re-use of disclosed material has
always been frowned upon by the courts. Indeed, in
the leading case on the point it was held that any
party receiving documents disclosed by order of a
court owed an obligation to that court not to make
collateral use of them. To quote from the judgment in
the case, if a party:

**Expert reports
cannot be re-used
unless permission
is obtained**

> *'can substantiate improper use in any*
> *particular case, he has his remedy. He can*
> *bring that instance of improper use before the*
> *court either on proceedings of contempt, if he*
> *considers that it amounts to contempt of court,*
> *or on proceedings to restrain the conduct*
> *complained of'.[7]*

Guidance for re-using expert reports

This safeguard for the owners of disclosed documents – and for present purposes that includes the authors of expert reports – now finds statutory expression in the CPR, although in a somewhat weaker form. CPR 31.22 provides that:

> *'(1) A party to whom a document has been*
> *disclosed may use the document only for the*
> *purpose of the proceedings in which it is*
> *disclosed, except where:*
>
> *(a) the document has been read to or by the*
> *court, or referred to, at a hearing which has*
> *been held in public;*
>
> *(b) the court gives permission; or*
>
> *(c) the party who disclosed the document and*
> *the person to whom the document belongs*
> *agree.'*

A report is disclosed once referred to in open court or read by judge

From this it is clear that once an expert report has been referred to in open court, or even has been read by the judge in chambers, it passes into the public domain. However, the Rule continues:

> *'(2) The court may make an order restricting or*
> *prohibiting the use of a document which has*
> *been disclosed, even where the document has*

---

[7] *Altersyke -v- Scott* [1948] 1 *AER* 469.

been read to or by the court, or referred to, at a hearing which has been held in public.

(3) An application for such an order may be made:

(a) by a party; or

(b) by any person to whom the document belongs.'

It follows that if an expert learns or suspects that a party to whom his report has been disclosed plans to make collateral use of it, then the expert can ask the court for a restraining order. Before doing that, though, it might be better for business if the expert contacted the party concerned and threatened to take this action unless a fee is paid for the report's re-use. To make such a proposal would require the prior agreement of the party for whom the report was originally written. Depending on the circumstances, though, it is an approach that could result in the expert being asked to prepare a fresh report for which an altogether bigger fee might be appropriate.

If re-use is planned, contact the party and request a fee – or else!

What CPR 31.22 fails to provide is any mechanism for redress after the event, apart from that of restricting or prohibiting further re-use. In circumstances where the re-use made is all that is likely to be made, the Rule affords no assistance to the aggrieved expert. In these circumstances, it seems, 'proceedings for contempt' are no longer an option. The expert might be able to sue for damages for breach of copyright, but that could prove an expensive undertaking and one that is by no means certain to succeed.

No mechanism for redress after the event

Suing for breach of copyright possible, but risky

What, though, if the offending party is the one for whom the report was originally prepared? Here, the CPR are no help whatsoever. For redress, the

Watertight contract and written instructions essential

aggrieved expert would have to rely on the contractual nature of his relationship with the solicitor concerned. Even if the latter's initial instructions were communicated verbally, they ought to have been confirmed in writing, and the written version should certainly have specified the case on which the expert was being instructed. In such circumstances there would be an implied undertaking on the solicitor's part not to use, or allow others to use, the expert report in proceedings other than those for which it was specifically written.

It always helps, of course, to be able to rely on an explicit undertaking rather than one that can only be implied. In this instance that is best achieved by the expert having terms of engagement which include a clause prohibiting collateral use of the report prepared.[8] Naturally enough, this leads on to the issue of copyright.

Copyright

Expert reports protected by copyright, including diagrams, tables, databases, etc.

Most of the materials experts create will be works protected by copyright. In the main, these will be classified as 'literary works'. This term covers any original written work (other than dramatic or musical work) and will include tables or compilations, computer programs, design specifications, reports and databases.

Other sorts of material produced by experts might attract copyright by virtue of their classification as original artistic works. For this purpose 'artistic works' are defined as including a graphic work, photograph, a work of architecture, being a building or model for a building, or a work of artistic craftsmanship. Examples of artistic works would

---

[8] See, for example, clause 4(h) in the outline set of Terms reproduced in *The Little Book on Expert Fees*.

include diagrams, charts, maps, graphic designs and photographs.

Ownership of copyright will vest in the **author** of the work. Section 9 of the Copyright, Designs and Patents Act 1988 defines 'author' simply as being the person who creates the work.

Copyright owned by the author, unless specified differently in the contract

Copyright confers:

- the moral rights to be identified as the author of the work (the right of 'paternity')
- the right to object to derogatory treatment of the work (the right to 'integrity')
- the right not to suffer false attribution
- the right to privacy in respect of certain films and photographs.

Generally, these rights last for the life of the author plus 70 years.

However, even in the case of original literary or artistic works, these moral rights do not apply in all circumstances. Reports produced by experts will, in normal circumstances, have been produced for a specific purpose and will be intended specifically for use by a third party.

A distinction needs to be made, however, between a contract *of* service and a contract *for* services. A contract of service will create an employer–employee relationship (essentially a contract of employment), whereas a contract for services is more likely to create a consultancy or contractor–subcontractor relationship.

If you are employed and the materials are produced in the course of your work for that employer, the employer will be the first owner of the copyright, subject to any agreement to the contrary. In those circumstances, ownership of copyright will become a

Employer owns copyright, unless special arrangements agreed

Consultancy outside normal work needs special contract relating to copyright, etc.

matter for contract. Works produced in the course of employment will normally vest copyright in the employer, but there are grey areas where precise ownership might be uncertain – for example, works produced outside normal working hours or relating to projects that are unrelated to the employer or outside the scope of the employment. For this reason, it is prudent for such contracts to include a specific intellectual property rights clause.

Stipulate copyright ownership in terms of engagement

A more common situation for experts will arise out of the contract for services where a report is commissioned directly from the expert. In the majority of cases the party commissioning the report will be a party to litigation, a solicitor or the court. In those circumstances the expert will retain the copyright, even though the commissioning party has paid for the work and 'bought' the report or other relevant work. This presumption is, however, subject to the terms of the contract.

In many cases, it will be an express or implied term of the contract that the commissioner will be entitled to the copyright. Provided the contract is enforceable, the commissioner will, in effect, be the equitable owner of the copyright, i.e. entitled to any profit arising from use of the material.[9] The contract may also be construed as an assignment of the intellectual property rights or, at least, a licence to use them.

Special rules apply to photographs

There are some specific statutory provisions that govern the copyright of commissioned photographs. The Copyright Act 1956 provides that where a person commissions a photograph, that person will, subject to certain conditions, be entitled to any subsisting copyright.

---

[9] *Lawrence & Bullen Ltd -v- Aflalo* [1904] 1 *AC* 17.

The normal assumptions of copyright ownership are, then, to some degree varied by the contractual arrangements under which the work is produced. Contractual terms can be either expressly agreed or implied from the nature of the contract or by custom. Accordingly, if an expert wishes to retain intellectual property rights, it is important that he should **spell these out** in the terms and conditions of accepting instructions.

For example, if the expert wishes to retain the rights to publish his report or extracts from it then it would be wise to expressly reserve this right when agreeing to carry out the work. Bear in mind, though, that what we are talking about here is the work itself and not the ideas it might contain. Copyright applies to the **form** in which the ideas are expressed – the ideas themselves are as free as air.

Think carefully about your possible other uses of the report

The Copyright, Designs and Patents Act 1988 does permit the assignment of copyrights in works that are, as yet, uncreated. This allows flexibility when agreeing contractual terms in advance of the work being carried out.

Copyright can be assigned to as yet uncreated works

If you are likely to want to claim copyright for your work, there are some basic steps you can take to protect it. UK law does not require any specific formalities to be observed, but you should:

Guidance for protecting your work

- **identify all materials** for which copyright is likely to be claimed
- **identify yourself** as the author of the work
- clarify any **ownership** and **licensing** issues
- if the work has been commissioned by a third party, ensure that there are **terms in place** to deal with assignment, licensing or any implied waiver of moral rights

- **keep proper records** of the above matters and **mark any documents** for which rights are claimed in accordance with the Universal Copyright Convention, i.e. © [name of copyright owner] [year of publication].

Confidentiality or privilege could limit re-use options

Having established copyright, however, there may be other considerations that will affect the expert's right to the free use and publication of the material. There are, of course, issues of confidentiality (particularly in relation to medical reports). Documents that have been produced in connection with legal proceedings may also attract privilege that would be breached by disclosure or publication. An expert would need to give careful consideration to these and, if in doubt, seek advice.

4

Meetings of Experts

Legal basis

Historically, the starting point in any discussion of the practice relating to expert meetings is a comment made by the judge trying the case of *Graigola Merthyr Co Ltd -v- Swansea Corporation.*[1] In the course of his judgment, Mr Justice Tomlin observed that:

Tomlin's observation went unheeded for many years

> *'Long cases produce evils... In every case of this kind there are generally many irreducible and stubborn facts upon which agreement between experts should be possible, and in my judgement the expert advisers of the parties, whether legal or scientific, are under a special duty to the court in the preparation of such a case to limit in every possible way the contentious matters of fact to be dealt with at the hearing. That is a duty which exists notwithstanding that it may not always be easy to discharge.'*

Unhappily, this comment went largely unheeded, for in the Interim Report of his Inquiry into the civil justice system, published in 1995, Lord Woolf concluded that the system was still failing to

---

[1] *Graigola Merthyr Co Ltd -v- Swansea Corporation* [1928] 1 *Ch* 31.

Woolf proposed greater use of expert meetings

encourage that need for narrowing of issues foreseen by Tomlin J almost 70 years previously. The solution recommended by Lord Woolf was that courts should insist on greater use being made of expert meetings.

Expert meetings usually ordered by the court

Expert meetings can take place at any time by arrangement between the parties to a dispute. It is more often the case, though, that they are ordered by the court, i.e. after proceedings have been issued. At the time of Lord Woolf's Inquiry, expert meetings frequently took place in technical and commercial cases in the high court, but less often in the county courts.

Most experts think expert meetings are worth while

The general view of those who have taken part in expert meetings is that they are 'a good thing'.[2] At the very least they serve to establish the extent of agreement and disagreement on technical issues, and they may help resolve some differences.

Identify common ground, highlight areas of dispute

In fact, it is quite likely that if the experts for both sides have been working from the same basic information, there will be much common ground. In such circumstances it should be possible for the experts to agree matters of fact without too much difficulty, while leaving areas of differing opinion, such as interpretation, degree and quantum, to be resolved. That, in turn, should enable the experts – and ultimately the court – to focus their attention on the issues that matter, with consequent savings in time and effort.

However, expert meetings can prove a complete waste of time if the experts taking part have been

---

[2] This is based on feedback gathered from the helpline of the *UK Register of Expert Witnesses* and from personal communications with experts attending various expert witness conferences.

told by their instructing solicitors not to agree anything without first obtaining clearance from them.

The attitude lawyers take towards expert meetings is often distinctly ambivalent:

- they **welcome the insight** such meetings can afford into the strengths and weaknesses of their own case and that of the opposing side

- but are **fearful of losing control** of any aspect of their client's case, however technical it might be.

Lawyers welcome insight but fear loss of control

There is also a perception that if, as Lord Woolf envisaged in his Final Report, expert meetings came to be ordered as a matter of routine, that could push up the costs of litigation, having a disproportionate effect on clients pursuing modest claims.

In fact, experience suggests the opposite: the majority of meetings are constructive and lead either to settlement before trial or to the agreement of substantial areas of common ground which can, in turn, reduce the time taken to give evidence and be cross-examined.

Most meetings are constructive and cost saving

Types of meeting

Meetings arranged by the parties

Parties adducing expert evidence have always been free to arrange between themselves meetings of their expert advisors. This has never become general practice because of the lawyer's desire to hide his hand until the last possible moment. Those meetings that are held generally take place in the context of negotiated settlements and often during the course of the trial.

Scope of meetings set up by the parties is defined by the parties

There are no rules governing expert meetings of this kind beyond those devised by the parties themselves.

- The scope of the meetings can be as narrow or as wide as the parties choose.
- The parties may give the experts as much authority as they like.

Ideally lawyers should not be present

It could be that the experts will be asked to settle a single technical issue, while at the other extreme they might be instructed to try to bring about a settlement. Although the instructing solicitors can, if they wish, arrange to be present throughout the meeting, this is generally undesirable because it tends to inhibit the freedom of dialogue between the experts and to restrict the effectiveness of their discussions. It is far better for the lawyers to impose a requirement that they be consulted before any agreement is concluded. In any event, it would be very unusual for experts to be authorised to conclude agreements that would bind the parties.

Experts must understand their brief and role

As meetings arranged by agreement are not governed by any Rules of Court or settled practice, it is especially important that the experts taking part in them ensure they are fully briefed as to the role they are to play. They will also need to inform the other experts present of any restrictions that have been placed upon their authority and whether or not their attendance is conditional on the proceedings being 'without prejudice'.

The remainder of this chapter will deal with the developing law and practice of court-ordered meetings of experts.

Court-ordered meetings

Aim of meetings to promote openness

Court-ordered meetings are a comparatively recent innovation. The practice of holding them originated in the Official Referees' Courts in the 1980s, although in those days such meetings could only take place with the consent of the parties. When courts were subsequently given the power to require that they be held, it was with the laudable aim of encouraging litigants to be more open about the merits of their cases.

The function of a court-ordered discussion is not negotiation. Indeed, it is never acceptable for an expert to shift his opinion purely to obtain a concession from the other expert. Such a discussion enables the experts to discuss the technical issues posed within their expertise, and to exchange opinions on them.

Discuss technical issues and exchange opinions

This discussion should result in:

- **clarification of the issues** the experts will need to address in their respective reports

- **pooling of technical information** regarding the case

- **identification of any gaps** in that information which may need to be filled, and

- **narrowing of the areas of difference**, some of which may at least be the result of a misunderstanding or lack of data.

Furthermore, experts taking part in court-ordered discussions should not be restrained by the parties instructing them from making a full contribution to the achievement of these aims. On the contrary, experts should show themselves willing to listen to other opinions and be prepared to revise their own in the light of what they learn. At the very least experts should try to identify the technical facts accepted by all sides, and those on which they cannot agree but have come to regard as peripheral.

Experts should be willing to listen and, if necessary, revise opinion

Identify accepted facts and unimportant disagreements

Rules and guidance

Civil Procedure Rules

Rules promote informal discussion to find common ground

These aims were taken a step further under the CPR that came into force in April 1999. The Rules speak of discussions between experts instead of meetings, and clearly envisage contacts of a more informal nature. The topic is tersely covered by Rule 35.12 (see page 188).

Important questions left unanswered – but see CJC Experts Protocol

However, the rule leaves unanswered the following important questions:

- Who may take part in the meeting?
- Who should prepare the agenda?
- Who should chair the meeting?
- What form should the required statement take?

The accompanying practice direction is no more helpful, being completely silent on the topic.

Experts may meet at any time during litigation

What is clear, though, is that:

- it is **entirely at the court's discretion** whether the procedure is invoked, and
- the court may require experts to **meet at any stage** in the litigation process.

In fast track, decision on expert meeting made at allocation

Given the tight timetabling of cases allocated to the fast track – only 30 weeks from allocation to trial – it is likely that for these the decision will have been made at the outset, i.e. at the allocation stage when the procedural judge decides whether to allow expert evidence at all.

All discussions privileged

The Rule also confirms the privileged nature of discussions that take place at court-ordered meetings of experts. At the same time, it makes clear that any statement experts may be required to draw up at the end of a meeting is for the court's use. It is an 'open' document. Although it may not be binding on the parties, it should prove invaluable to the court in its subsequent management of the case.

Expert agreement not binding unless parties agree

The 'open' nature of the statement has one other major consequence. An expert witness could hardly submit evidence to a court that was contrary to what had been agreed at a meeting of experts ordered by the court – unless, that is, new information had come to hand to justify a change of mind. This could place the instructing party in a real quandary if it is unwilling to abide by the statement of issues agreed at the expert meeting.

Subsequent evidence must conform to agreed statement unless new evidence appears

In a multi-track case the party might be able to persuade the court to allow it to instruct a new expert and to order a fresh meeting of experts. In that event, however, it would certainly have to meet the costs of the first expert regardless of the outcome of the case. It is most unlikely, though, that such an application could succeed in a fast-track case, for it would completely wreck the case's timetable. All the more reason, then, why the practical aspects of expert meetings deserve the most careful attention of everyone involved in either arranging or attending them.

What if the parties are unhappy with the agreed statement?

Fortunately, some of the issues left open by the Rules are addressed in section 18 of the CJC *Experts Protocol* which came into effect in September 2005 (see page 208).

Experts Protocol

Directions

It is for the court to decide whether to order a meeting of experts. In the exercise of its case management function it may do so at any stage in the proceedings. Most usually, though, the order will

Meetings can be ordered at any stage, but usually at allocation

be one of the directions issued at the time the case is allocated to a track.

Timing of meeting at discretion of the court

It is also for the court to decide when the meeting should take place. It may require that the experts meet before exchange of their reports or after exchange. Alternatively, the court may leave the timing of the meeting to be settled by the parties.

Court may specify issues in detail

Similarly, the order can be quite detailed about the issues the experts are to address, or mention none at all.

Fast-track cases cause timetabling problems

Should a meeting be ordered in a fast-track case, one problem that may well arise is that of scheduling within the tight timetable prescribed for such cases. As a general rule, the hearing of a fast-track case has to take place within 30 weeks of it being allocated to the track. If the parties have not already exchanged expert reports, they would normally be ordered to do so no later than 14 weeks from allocation.

Who takes part?

Not all experts may be called upon to meet

Experts obviously take part in expert meetings, but they are not necessarily joined by all of those involved in the case. Where experts have been instructed to deal with different aspects, the court may order meetings of 'experts of like discipline'. On grounds of cost alone there are clear advantages in that.

Clinical negligence a special case

On the other hand, while this limitation will be desirable in most cases, it may not be so in all of them. For example, in actions for clinical negligence it has been found that when experts on breach of duty and those on causation meet, the interchange of views can go a long way towards determining where the real issues in the case lie.

Should lawyers be present?

The CJC *Experts Protocol* states that lawyers will not be present 'unless all the parties and their experts otherwise agree or a court so orders'. If present, lawyers should only answer questions put to them by the experts or advise about the law.

Lawyers not present unless all parties agree or ordered by the court

In this respect, the *Protocol* clearly reflects the widely held view that if lawyers were to attend, some experts could be inhibited from making a full and frank contribution to the discussion, perhaps out of concern that the ideas they float might be used against them in cross-examination. Although the Rules provide that anything said in the course of an expert meeting may not be referred to in court, it still leaves open the possibility that a lawyer listening to the discussion might glean from it additional ways of probing an expert's evidence and undermining his confidence in the witness box.

Presence of lawyers can inhibit frank discussions

Against this, it has to be said that expert discussions can get derailed easily for other reasons. For example:

Lawyers can be useful to maintain focus

- an inexperienced expert so far defers to the views of the other expert in the case as to completely abandon the opinions advanced in his original report
- both experts may be so inclined to compromise that the agreed statement produced fails to reflect the views of either of them
- one or both experts may assume the role of advocate for the client and even usurp the function of the court in deciding where blame lies in the case.

In all these circumstances, if the lawyers for the parties were present at the meeting, they would (hopefully) intervene to prevent such an outcome and get the discussion back on track.

Litigators want input to represent the client

One further point made by litigation lawyers is that it is they, not the experts, who represent the interests of their clients. In their view it is wholly unreasonable that the outcome of a case should be determined, as it is quite often, by a statement produced at the end of an unmonitored discussion between two experts, one of whom may well not have met their client and who, in the context of legal proceedings, owe the client only a secondary duty of care. If the lawyers were present at the discussion, even though they are debarred from taking part in it, they could at least exercise a watching brief on their client's behalf.

When should the meetings be held?

Experts want meetings held as early as possible

As we have seen, the court itself may require that the ordered meeting of experts takes place before or after exchange of their reports. The circumstances of the case and the facts to be established by expert evidence largely determine which stage is preferred. Given the choice, most experts would like meetings to take place sooner rather than later. If experts can agree the issues not in contention early on, then they need not cover them in any detail in the reports yet to be written. That, in turn, should reduce the amount of material the court has to consider and ultimately costs.

Fast-track timetabling causes problems

However, arranging meetings before reports have been finalised can cause particular problems in fast-track cases: tight timetabling normally requires the reports to be exchanged within 14 weeks of allocation to that track.

Discussions need not be face to face

This is one reason, no doubt, why Rule 35.12 refers to 'discussions' rather than 'meetings': it clearly implies that they need not be face to face. The CJC

Experts Protocol requires that arrangements for discussions should be proportionate to the value of the case. So in small claim and fast-track cases a telephone discussion or exchange of letters will normally suffice.

On the other hand, and especially in complicated cases assigned to the multi-track, opportunities for meaningful discussions may be missed if the experts meet before they have all had the chance to complete their own investigations and at least draft a preliminary report. To attend a meeting without having any prior knowledge of the technical basis of the opposing side's case can prove very frustrating.

Complicated multi-track cases require more preparation pre-meeting

There can be even greater disadvantages, though, in requiring experts to meet after their final reports have been exchanged.

Meeting after exchange disadvantageous

- Experts will have completed their investigations by that stage (and, quite conceivably, incurred most of their expenses).
- Experts are likely to be less willing to change opinions expressed in their reports, either out of embarrassment at having to acknowledge the superiority of another viewpoint or because the reports will by then have been accepted by their clients as the basis on which to proceed.
- In the event of the meeting achieving its purpose, there will be a need to apply to the court for permission for the experts to amend their reports or submit supplementary versions. It may even become necessary to amend the statement of claim – all of which could delay proceedings.

Given these circumstances, perhaps the best to be hoped for in multi-track cases is that a more-or-less standard form of order emerges:

Ideally dates set for initial exchange, expert meeting and final exchange

- requiring the exchange of *initial* reports by a specified date
- setting another date by which the experts are to meet
- fixing the date by which trial, or final, reports are to be exchanged.

Where should they be held?

Convenient location most important

The principal consideration in choosing the venue for a face-to-face meeting of experts is that it should be **convenient for the majority** of those attending. It could be held at the offices of one of the experts, and perhaps most suitably at those of the claimant's expert (during the early stages of litigation it is likely that the claimant's expert will have assembled the fuller range of documentation).

Preparation

Agreed agenda essential

If expert meetings are to fulfil their purpose, it is essential that experts work to an agenda agreed in advance. The CJC *Experts Protocol* states that 'the parties, their lawyers and experts should co-operate to produce' the agenda.

Claimant lawyer usually draws up agenda, with expert input

At one time it was often the case that the claimant's expert drew up the agenda for any meeting with colleagues instructed by the other side. Nowadays, though, it is much more likely that the initiative will come from the claimant's lawyer, perhaps with input from the claimant's expert. Moreover, in negligence cases, at least, it is probably necessary that lawyers should take the lead in this way, given the complexity of the legal tests for establishing causation.

Conduct of the meeting

The detailed arrangements for holding an expert meeting are normally left to the experts themselves.

If more than two experts are present, it is advisable that one should act as the chairperson. Whoever acts as the chair would be wise to conduct the proceedings in as relaxed and informal a manner as the circumstances allow. If, however, the meeting is following an agenda or *aide memoire* prepared by one of the claimant's experts, the chairperson must ensure that each of the other experts present is called upon to speak and given every opportunity to do so.

Informality breeds openness

Every expert must be invited to contribute

Even when meetings are held before exchange of trial reports it will often be the case that those taking part will have formed conclusions as to the fundamental issues between the parties. It may be unrealistic to expect them to abandon these opinions at the meeting. In such circumstances, another way to proceed is to adopt the 'what if' approach. Experts should attempt to agree the factual basis for the rival views along the lines of 'If A applies then we agree Y will follow, but if B applies we agree that Z will follow'. This at least has the merit of recognising that should the case reach court, either A or B is going to be preferred.

If agreement can't be reached, try the 'what if' approach

Occasionally, those attending meetings of experts will find that one of their number adopts a hostile or unco-operative stance. If that attitude persists, it could ruin any chances of a successful outcome. It is then incumbent on the others present to overcome the problem as far as possible and to attempt to win that expert round. Most individuals will respond to tactful handling and a show of flexibility on the part of their fellow professionals. So experts need to be prepared to concede points in the face of intransigence. Another tack might be to abandon the agenda and concentrate on those issues most easily resolved, hoping thereby to progress to the more

Intransigent experts need tactful handling

Start with easily resolved issues, then move on to more difficult ones

difficult ones when some measure of mutual respect has been gained.

Keep minutes, draw up an agreed statement

What is essential, even if the court has not required it, is that minutes are kept of the discussion. If at all possible, a statement should be drawn up at the end of the meeting setting out the experts's answers to the questions posed by the agenda and signed and dated by all present.

Give reasons for agreement and disagreement

Rule 35.12(3) lays down that a statement must detail those issues on which the experts agree and those on which they disagree, with a summary of their reasons for disagreeing. But the CJC *Experts Protocol* goes further. It requires, for example, that reasons should be given for agreement on issues, as well as for disagreement. At first glance this might seem otiose, but it presumably reflects the desire to allay the suspicions of the clients that they might have been 'stitched up' by experts who are too concerned not to offend colleagues by disagreeing on crucial points. In addition, the CJC *Experts Protocol* requires that the statement should include a list of further issues identified during the discussion but not on the agenda, and a record of any further action the experts agreed was needed to resolve these and any other outstanding issues.

Include list of further issues identified plus action needed

Joint statement must be signed by all experts at meeting

The CJC *Experts Protocol* requires any joint statement to be agreed and signed by the experts taking part in the discussion as soon as practicable. If this can be done at the meeting, then all well and good. For practical reasons, though, that may not always be feasible. In that event, it will be the responsibility of the expert chairing the meeting to circulate a draft statement to the others for their approval and signature. To avoid uncertainty as to who agreed to what at any meeting where many issues are due to be covered, it is a sensible precaution for the chairperson to ensure that those

All experts should initial each minute

taking part initial the minute taken of the discussion **on each issue**. In this way it should be possible to prepare a draft statement quickly that will secure the prompt approval of everyone concerned.

Status of the joint statement

As has already been noted, court-ordered meetings are 'without prejudice'. Nothing said or agreed at them in any way binds the parties to the dispute. But what of the joint written statement which Rule 35.12 and the CJC *Experts Protocol* require the experts to prepare? One school of thought maintains that once the experts have committed to paper their agreement on anything, the matters thus covered become binding on the experts's principals, particularly if the written statement isn't clearly marked 'without prejudice'.

> **Court-ordered meetings are without prejudice and not binding**

That, however, flies in the face of reason on two counts. First, as Judge John Newey noted in the leading case of *Richard Roberts Holdings Ltd -v- Douglas Smith Stimson*[3], it is:

> **But how binding is the signed statement?**

'*... alien to the role of expert witnesses that they should have an automatic power to bind [anyone]. An expert does not represent a party in the way that a solicitor represents his client; he is principally a witness and his duties are to explain to the court (and no doubt those who instruct him) technical matters and to give objective 'opinion' evidence.*'

> **Experts do not represent the client**

Second, agreements recorded by experts may be worded in ways that have legal consequences they, as non-lawyers, could hardly be expected to foresee. On that ground, too, the legal advisors of the parties must have the opportunity to consider and amend any agreement recorded in a joint statement of

> **Experts may unknowingly use words with legal implications**

---

[3] *Richard Roberts Holdings Ltd -v- Douglas Smith Stimson Partnership* [1988] 46 *BLR* 50.

experts before it can be considered to have a binding effect.

Expert's position subsequent to the meeting

Nothing discussed or agreed can be disclosed in court

What is quite clear is that nothing discussed or agreed during the course of a 'without prejudice' meeting of experts may be disclosed in court. It follows that should an expert who has taken part in such a meeting come to give his evidence in court, the expert cannot be cross-examined about the discussions or, more to the point, any inconsistencies between the evidence-in-chief and what may have been stated or agreed at the meeting.

Experts cannot be cross-examined about discussions

That said, it would clearly be wrong for an expert to give evidence at trial contrary to what was previously said or agreed at a meeting of experts – unless, that is, fresh evidence has been discovered or a genuine change of mind has occurred.

Position of the party

What if the expert agrees to matters contrary to the party's case?

By the same token, the party whose expert agrees at a 'without prejudice' meeting matters contrary to that party's pleaded case has very limited options.

- The party may choose to **concede all or part of its case**.
- The party can **seek leave to amend its statement of claim**.
- The party can **dispense with the services of its expert**.

Clearly, this last option becomes more difficult the nearer the case is to trial. It also has financial implications in that the instructing solicitor would then have to ask the court to order a second expert meeting in the almost certain knowledge that the client would be made totally liable for the costs of the first meeting regardless of the eventual outcome of the case.

Either way, there is a real possibility of the client suffering loss as a result of the expert's actions at the meeting. If this were to occur, the client might well be tempted to sue the expert for negligence. However, following the Court of Appeal decision in the case of *Stanton -v- Callaghan*[4], such an action is most unlikely to succeed.[5]

Conclusion

Court-ordered meetings serve as follows:

- to **focus the attention** of both the experts and those instructing them on the technical issues that really matter
- to **narrow the issues in dispute**, and
- to **promote early settlement** of the case.

Even when settlement does not occur, such meetings should at least result in the experts producing shorter, better focused reports, with all the consequent savings in court time that will follow. Since cost has always been one of the principal bugbears of civil litigation, this alone would be sufficient justification for the wider use of expert meetings as envisaged by Lord Woolf in his Final Report.

Expert meetings lead to savings in court time and costs

---

[4] *Stanton -v- Callaghan* [1998] 4 *AER* 961.

[5] For a discussion of this case, see *Chapter 9: Immunity from Suit.*

5 Answering Questions

The CPR require at Rule 35.1 that 'expert evidence shall be restricted to that which is reasonably required to resolve the proceedings'. Rule 35.4 ensures that this objective is achieved by placing the calling of expert evidence under the complete control of the court, while Rule 35.5 provides that evidence shall be given in a written report 'unless the court directs otherwise'.

Clearly, though, there are dangers in a court receiving a written report that has not been scrutinised for inconsistencies or ambiguities – especially when, as is often the case nowadays, there will be no opportunity to cross-examine the expert at a later stage in the proceedings. Hence, the countervailing provisions of Rule 35.6 that enable parties to seek clarification of an expert's report by means of written questions, the answers to which will then form part of the report.

Parties can seek clarification of expert reports by written questions

CPR provisions

The main purpose of the CPR *Written questions to experts* procedure (set out in CPR 35.6 and the supplementary provisions contained in the Practice Direction 35.5) is to help parties understand the reports disclosed to them by their opponents. If, however, questions are put that are oppressive in

Court warns lawyers against abusing the Rule – cost orders threatened

number or content, or if – without the permission of the court or the agreement of the other side – questions are asked for any purpose other than clarification of an expert report, the guidance warns that 'the court will not hesitate to disallow the questions and to make an appropriate order for costs against the party putting them'.

Rule in practice

For such a simple and straightforward procedure it is surprising how often experts and lawyers experience problems. Indeed, to judge from their comments, some believe it to be not so much used as abused.

Excessive questions not unusual

At the *UK Register of Expert Witnesses* we first became aware of this in February 2000, following a survey we conducted of the experiences of our readers while acting as SJEs.[1] Of 60 respondents who had by then been instructed as SJEs at least 10 times, nine thought that the questions asked were generally excessive. One surveyor had received no fewer than 54 questions put to him about one of his reports, while an occupational therapist had notched up 76 questions on one of hers. There are, however, special considerations concerning the questioning of SJEs that will be touched on later.

It is not just our readers of *Your Witness* who have encountered problems with the procedure. Instances have been reported in other journals of experts receiving several successive batches of questions. Others have had questions sent to them months after their reports were exchanged. And at least one expert claims to have been asked questions in pursuance of the Rule by telephone!

---

[1] Reported in *Your Witness* 23 published by J S Publications. Surf to www.jspubs.com for further details or call 01638 561590.

Excessive and onerous questions

It cannot be stressed too strongly that Rule 35.6 was never intended to provide a substitute for cross-examination, still less a means for intimidating an opponent's expert. However, the issue of what constitutes excessive or onerous questioning has yet to be tested in court. When it is, the decision will almost certainly be dependent on whether the court regards the questions as 'proportionate'. In other words, were they justified in view of:

Are the questions 'proportionate'?

- the **amount of money** at stake
- the **importance** of the case
- the **complexity** of the issues, or
- the **relative financial position** of the parties?

Clearly, these are matters for lawyers to assess, not experts. This is why we believe it best that experts leave it to the lawyers to decide how to deal with an apparent abuse of the procedure.

Leave it to the lawyers to sort out!

There are various courses of action open to a lawyer whose expert has been sent questions that seem excessive in number or otherwise impermissible. He can:

- **remonstrate** with the solicitor who sent them
- **apply to the court** to have the questions disallowed, or
- **accept the situation** and instruct the expert to answer the questions – which is the most likely course if the solicitor suspects that the court may be glad to have the additional information anyway.

There is no need at all for experts to take it upon themselves to apply to the court for directions.

Special considerations for lawyers

In dealing with written questions, two considerations will be uppermost in the minds of the lawyers on both sides: cost and delay.

Cost

Instructing lawyer pays expert to answer questions from opposition

The Part 35 Practice Direction requires that when an expert answers questions put in accordance with Rule 35.6, it is his instructing party (and, in practice, that means instructing solicitor) who must pay the expert for answering them. At first sight this may seem odd, but it is in fact sensible: the two are already in a contractual relationship and will have – or, at least, should have – agreed the basis on which the expert is to charge his fees.

Costs recoverable if case is won

Costs may be recoverable if case is lost

In any event, as the Practice Direction also reminds us, this does not mean that the client will necessarily foot the bill. If the case is won, the cost of answering the questions should be recoverable from the party that put them. Even if the case is lost, the winning party could still be ordered to reimburse the loser for the cost of having questions answered if the court found them to be excessive or otherwise unreasonable.

Delay

What effect will asking questions have on keeping to the timetable?

Nowadays the great majority of cases – perhaps as many as 80% – are allocated to the fast track. For cases on that track, no more than 30 weeks should elapse between allocation and trial. Typically, the court will require that expert reports be exchanged within 14 weeks of allocation, leaving just 16 weeks for the lawyers to complete all remaining stages.

Fast-track timetabling adds pressure

Let's consider for a moment what that involves. The party receiving the report of its opponent's expert has 4 weeks in which to consider it, consult its own expert about any aspects it does not understand and, if necessary (and with that expert's help), frame questions to put to the author of the report. Then, if the party is lucky, it will receive replies to its questions in another month, by which time the trial date may be only 8 weeks away. All this should, as they say, concentrate minds wonderfully on keeping questions short and to the point, and on not asking more than are absolutely necessary.

Meaning of 'clarification'

Clause (2) of Rule 35.6 ends with an important proviso that is still, on occasion, overlooked by litigants and their advisors. It enables written questions to be put:

With permission, questions can be put more than once

- more than once

- more than 28 days after reports have been exchanged, and

- for purposes other than clarification

if the court gives permission or the other party agrees.

Exactly what kind of question might be permitted that goes beyond clarification was the issue before the Court of Appeal in *Mutch -v- Allen* (see page 122). The Court ruled that a judge is entitled to be provided with all the evidence relevant to his decision in the most cost-effective and expeditious way. To that end, it is legitimate for a party to ask questions of an expert witness in **extension**, as well as clarification, of his report. This is so provided the question deals with a material point the witness did not cover in the report, even though it was within his expertise.

Questions in extension of a report can also be asked, but only with permission

Always seek permission first

Ask your instructing lawyer before answering questions from another party

Clearly, the issues involved in answering questions are not quite as straightforward as they might seem from a quick reading of Rule 35.6 or the associated provisions of the Part 35 Practice Direction. For that reason, the advice to experts is that, other than in the most trivial circumstances, experts should *always* establish that they have their instructing solicitor's permission before answering any questions from another party on a report they have written.

When questions arrive with written instructions

Keep your instructing lawyer informed of likely extra costs

If the questions have been submitted via the instructing solicitor and have been forwarded with a request that the expert respond to them, all well and good. Even here, though, there is a possibility that the solicitor may not have appreciated just how much additional work will be entailed in answering them. In such circumstances the solicitor may well appreciate a quick note enclosing an estimate of the time it will take to comply with the request and a reminder of the expert's fee rate. That should produce an equally prompt response either confirming or countermanding the previous instruction.

When questions arrive without instruction or direct from another party

Ensure the instructing lawyer is fully aware of the content

The need to seek permission to answer questions is even greater if questions have been forwarded by or on behalf of an instructing solicitor without specific instructions, or if they have come direct from the questioning party. Although the Practice Direction requires any question sent direct to an expert to be copied to the party or parties by whom he has been instructed, that does not always happen. Without checking, there is always a risk that the instructing solicitor may neither have seen the questions, nor considered the implications of the expert answering them, before the expert begins work.

Answering questions

Once the expert has been given the go ahead, the task of answering the questions should be started as quickly as possible. If the case is on the fast track, though, time will already be pressing. The parties would doubtless appreciate a faster turnaround.

Fast track demands quick turn around

If the expert should anticipate any difficulty in replying within a suitable timescale, both parties should be advised of the estimated delay. They can then be left to consider whether to make a joint application to the court for postponement of the trial date.

Inform parties immediately if delay likely

Experts should always bear in mind that answers to questions put in accordance with Rule 35.6 automatically form part of the expert report. They are therefore covered by the statement of truth included in that report. In particular, answers must represent the expert's 'true and complete professional opinion'. For similar reasons, experts should be wary of allowing their answers to betray any of the irritation or annoyance they may feel about being asked to 'clarify' a report they regard as crystal clear. It is for the court to decide whether the questions were necessary and, if it sees fit, to penalise the party that asked them.

Remember, written answers form part of the final report

Finally, when the answers are ready, they should be sent direct to the party that put them. In addition, two copies should be sent to the expert's instructing solicitor, with the request that one of these be forwarded to the court. The expert will no doubt wish to submit at the same time an invoice for the additional work done.

Send answers direct to questioner and copies to instructing lawyer

117

Single joint experts: a special case

Written questions can be put to SJEs

Rule 35.6 provides that a party may put written questions to an SJE about his report, just as it may to an expert appointed by another party alone. In both cases the questions:

- may be **put only once**
- must be **put within 28 days** of service of the report, and
- can only be **in clarification** of the report

unless the court gives permission or the instructing parties agree otherwise.

Questions must be copied to all parties

The Practice Direction further requires that if a party sends such questions direct to the SJE, it must at the same time copy them to the solicitors representing the other parties.

The difficulties with this provision are two-fold:

- the meaning of 'clarification', and
- the lack of any restriction on the number of questions that may be put.

Particular difficulties for SJEs

While these are difficulties that may be experienced by any expert, they are likely to bear more heavily on SJEs since they are liable to be questioned in this way by both sides. Furthermore, several instances have been reported of SJEs being sent aggressively worded questions in an attempt to bludgeon them into changing their reports to reflect the questioner's viewpoint. Other SJEs have told of their receiving sheaves of questions that could take as much time to answer as the report itself took to prepare.

Do not answer questions until agreement of all parties received

If an SJE believes that the questions put about the report are seeking more than clarification of its meaning, or if it seems that they are excessive in number, then **concerns should be raised with all**

the instructing parties simultaneously. At the same time, the SJE should provide the parties with an estimate of the number of extra hours of work that answering the questions would entail and remind them of the hourly fee rate. Then, if one party should object to incurring the additional cost, it can be relied upon to take the matter up with the other parties. In all events, the SJE should not answer the questions causing concern until the agreement of all the parties has been given.

Pre-action reports

Part 35 of the CPR is concerned solely with the use of expert evidence **once proceedings have been issued**. Whether such evidence is needed at an earlier stage – and, if so, how it is to be obtained – is for the parties to determine, though with some guidance from pre-action protocols. What, then, is the position with regard to the questioning of reports commissioned during the pre-action stage of a dispute?

Advisory reports

If an expert should be instructed to prepare a report for the information of one party and that party alone, no issues arise. The report would be purely advisory. The questions could only come from the party that commissioned it and – like the report itself – any exchange of questions and answers about it would be privileged to that party.

Advisory reports are commissioned for one side only and answers are privileged

Pre-action protocols

Where problems have occurred is with the questioning of reports prepared in pursuance of a pre-action protocol. The main purposes of such protocols are:

119

- to **secure the early exchange of information** about a prospective claim, and

- **to facilitate settlement** should proceedings commence.

Appointment of single expert encouraged

It is left largely to the parties to decide whether expert evidence would help them achieve these objectives. But if they agree that it would, then they are encouraged to consider commissioning a single expert to produce the report they need.

Careful!
Joint selection is NOT joint instruction

Careful!
Report is privileged

It is important to note, though, that while it is necessarily the case that such an expert will have been jointly selected by the parties, it does not follow that he must, or even should, be jointly *instructed* by them. That may be the ideal situation, but the protocol for personal injury claims, for example, specifically provides that only one party (generally the claimant) shall instruct the agreed expert. This has an important consequence for the conduct of such claims, because privilege then attaches to the report the expert produces. As a result, the instructing party will be under no obligation to disclose it to the opponents. Indeed, if the instructing side does not like the report, the party may simply discard it and start all over again.

Let's assume, though, that the agreed expert report *has* been disclosed, and any privilege over it thereby waived. Both parties may then submit written questions to its author.

Questions must be 'relevant'

In the more relaxed regime that pertains at this stage of personal injury litigation, the only precondition is that the questions asked should be relevant. Indeed, none of the protocols approved so far specifies a time limit, either for putting the questions or for answering them.

The personal injury protocol does differ from the others, though, in stipulating the way in which the expert is to respond to questions received: the answers have to be sent separately and directly to the party that put them. This underlines a distinction that no expert in a personal injury case can afford to ignore. **An 'agreed' expert is one that has been jointly selected, not jointly instructed.**

PI protocol states responses to be sent to questioner only

Only when an expert has been jointly instructed does he owe both parties that duty of fairness and transparency which should govern the conduct of SJEs appointed after proceedings have commenced.

It follows that an 'agreed' expert in a personal injury case should never fall into the trap of assuming that he ought to be keeping each party informed of questions received from the other or be supplying them with copies of the answers sent. The answers are privileged to the party that asked the questions.

Answers privileged to party asking questions

One final point. Unlike the procedure for questioning reports exchanged later on, the costs of an expert answering questions during the pre-action stage will usually be borne by the party asking them. This is logical because if the protocol being followed achieves its purpose, the dispute may settle there and then. In that event each side will be responsible for meeting its own costs.

Each party responsible for fees of expert answering their own questions

Experts instructed in accordance with a pre-action protocol should ensure that their terms of agreement take account of this situation. Ideally, experts should require that their instructing solicitor pays them for answering all the questions forwarded, leaving the solicitor to recover such sums from the other parties as may be appropriate.

Terms should account for answering questions

Meaning of 'clarification'

What constitutes clarification?

According to Rule 35.6(2), the only ground for which a party may put questions to an expert about his report is for the purpose of clarification – unless, that is, the court permits them to range more widely or the other party agrees to them doing so. However, exactly what constitutes 'clarification'? The question was answered decisively by the Court of Appeal in a case decided in March 2001.[2]

The facts of *Mutch -v- Allen* are straightforward enough. The claimant was injured in an accident while travelling as a backseat passenger in a car driven by the defendant. He was not wearing a seat belt at the time, and on account of this the defendant alleged contributory negligence. If that were proven, and depending, of course, on causation, it could have reduced the eventual award by 50% or more.

Questions put in extension to the report, not clarification

In his report, the claimant's principal expert, a Professor Solomon, noted that the claimant was not wearing a seat belt, but said nothing of the consequences of his failure to do so. After some considerable delay, the defendant's solicitors wrote to Professor Solomon to ask whether the severity of the claimant's injuries would have been reduced, if not altogether prevented, had he been wearing a seat belt. They also asked which injuries might have been lessened or avoided in that event.

Claimant lawyer objected, but request overruled

The letter was copied to the claimant's solicitors who straightaway objected to the questions and instructed Professor Solomon not to answer them. When, however, the point was taken at a case management conference, their objections were overruled and the request to the claimant's expert was renewed. In due course, the expert confirmed to

---

[2] *Mutch -v- Allen* [2001] *EWCA Civ* 76; [2001] *CP* 77.

both parties that in his opinion the claimant's injuries would indeed have been much less severe if a seat belt had been worn. In particular, he would not have suffered the very severe fracture to his pelvis sustained on being thrown from the car.

The trial of the action was fixed for February 2001, but at a pre-trial review Judge Hutton, sitting as a High Court judge, accepted counsel's submission that the questions put to the claimant's expert went beyond clarification of his report and for that reason neither they nor the answers to them should be placed before the trial judge.

Pre-trial review ruled questions and answers inadmissible

This was a double-whammy for the defendant, because in the expectation of being able to rely on Professor Solomon's answers, he had not sought permission to instruct an orthopaedic expert of his own and now had insufficient time to do so. Not surprisingly, then, he sought to have the decision reversed in the Court of Appeal.

As Lord Justice Simon Brown dryly observed while delivering the Court's lead judgment, there could be little doubt that had those answers been more favourable to the claimant's case they would have been enthusiastically adopted by him. The issue was, being disappointed in that regard, could he properly seek to have the answers annulled on the ground that, as Judge Hutton had put it, ' the claimant does not have to prove the defendant's case'?

His Lordship then quoted with approval a footnote in *The White Book* concerning Rule 35.6, which reads:

'This is a most useful provision… it enables a party to obtain clarification of a report prepared by an expert instructed by his opponent or to arrange for a point not covered in the report (but within his expertise) to be dealt with. In a given case, were it

Appeal judge noted clarification and extension of report allowed

not possible to achieve such clarification or extension of the report, the court, for that reason alone, may feel obliged to direct that the expert witness should testify at trial.'

Had Professor Solomon been called to give evidence for the reason cited there, the defendant would almost certainly have taken the opportunity to ask the same questions in cross-examination. Equally plainly, he would have been entitled to rely on the answers then given to prove his case.

The judge at first instance had erred in failing to recognise that expert medical evidence on the issue of causation, namely the effect that not wearing a seat belt had on the severity of the claimant's injuries, was not only relevant but of the greatest materiality to the outcome of the case. He had also overlooked the fundamental purpose of CPR Part 35, which is to ensure that experts no longer serve the exclusive interest of those who retain them, but rather contribute to a just disposal of disputes by making their expertise available to all. In the instant case, both the questions put to the claimant's expert and his answers to them were admissible as part of his evidence, even though they manifestly rebounded to the defendant's advantage.

The lesson of this Court of Appeal decision is clear. A court is entitled to be provided with all relevant matter in the most cost-effective and expeditious way. To that end, it is legitimate to ask questions of an expert in extension, as well as clarification, of his report.

6 The Hearing

Experts who provide reports will not always have to appear in court. In a great many cases their reports will have been agreed and, consequently, they will not be called upon to attend a hearing. Indeed it is becoming more and more uncommon for experts to be examined and cross-examined on their evidence.

Court appearance is rare, and getting rarer!

It is entirely possible, then, that an expert might work for some time before experiencing the delights (or otherwise) of a personal court appearance. Those unfamiliar with the workings of the court should prepare for this by making themselves fully aware of court etiquette and the rules governing the giving of evidence.

When your time comes, familiarise yourself well in advance

Rules of etiquette

Courtroom etiquette is the same for expert witnesses as for any other person using or appearing in the court. Broadly speaking these are merely rules of good behaviour and can be summarised as follows:

Basics of courtroom etiquette

- **Remove all headgear** before entering the court. (There are exceptions for religious observances.)
- **Enter and leave the courtroom at an appropriate time** so as to cause as little disturbance as possible.

- When the judge comes into court and bows to the court, everyone bows back – as a mark of respect. A small **bow of the head** is sufficient.
- When not giving evidence, **keep quiet** at all times.
- **Sit in the designated area**, which will be pointed out to you by the usher.
- **Stand when the judge enters or leaves** the courtroom.
- Always **ask the usher if you are in any doubt** as to what to do.
- The following activities are not permitted in court: smoking, eating and drinking, reading magazines and newspapers, taking photographs, making tape-recordings, using a mobile phone, using a personal stereo, bringing an animal into court – except a guide dog accompanying a registered blind person.

Forms of address

Address the judge correctly; if in doubt, clarify with your instructing lawyer

It is a common misconception that all members of the judiciary are addressed in court as 'your honour'. In fact, most are not.

- **District judges** sitting in the County Courts or Magistrates Courts should be addressed as *Sir* or *Madam*.
- **Asylum and Immigration Tribunal judges** and **chairmen of other tribunals** should be addressed as *Sir* or *Madam*.
- **Magistrates** can be addressed as *Sir* or *Madam* or as *Your Worship*.
- **High Court Masters** should be addressed as *Master* (whether they are male or female).
- **Registrars** are addressed as *Registrar*.
- **High Court Judges** are referred to as *My Lord* or *My Lady*.

- For **Appeal Court Judges** use *My Lord* or *My Lady*.
- It is only **Circuit Judges** who are addressed as *Your Honour*. Even here, there are exceptions to the rule. For example, Central Criminal Court judges and some other circuit judges (like the Recorder of Liverpool) are traditionally addressed as *My Lord* or *My Lady* rather than as *Your Honour*.

Avoid excessive use of these terms, however. It is probably sufficient to use them once to preface or end your responses. It would be inappropriate – and, frankly, laborious – to use them in every sentence.

Avoid overuse of these forms of address

Taking the oath

You will be called by the court usher and will be asked to stand while reading out the words of the oath from a card. No talking is permitted while the witness is being sworn. The taking of the oath is viewed by the court as a grave matter.

Taking of the oath is a grave matter

The Oaths Act 1978 makes provisions for the forms in which oaths may be administered. It states that a solemn affirmation to tell the truth shall be of the same force and effect as an oath sworn on a holy book. In today's inclusive multi-cultural society all citizens, whether or not they are members of faith traditions, should be treated sensitively when making affirmations or declarations, or when swearing oaths.

Format of the oath flexible

As with other witnesses, the expert remains under oath until discharged by the judge. At the conclusion of the evidence the judge will release and thank the expert, who is then free to go. But remember...

Expert remains under oath until discharged

- The **expert should not discuss the case** with people outside the court.

Expert usually required to remain in court

- The **expert will usually be required to assist his instructing legal team**. This will frequently mean sitting behind counsel whilst the other side's expert gives evidence, and answering any questions that may arise. Experts will need to explain often quite basic things about that evidence and will need to stay alert for any inaccuracies it might contain.

Examination-in-chief

The sequence in which the civil and criminal courts hear evidence is broadly the same.

Claimant's case first, defendant's case second

Following opening submissions from the parties, the party bringing the case (variously called the claimant, applicant or plaintiff) will present its case and call its witnesses to give evidence. The party defending the case (variously called the defendant or respondent) will then give its evidence.

Witnesses can be called in any order

There is no set order in which a party is obliged to call their witnesses. However, given that the evidence must follow some logical narrative sequence, it is probable that the witnesses as to fact will be called first, followed by the expert evidence.

Instructing advocate questions the expert first

When the expert witness is called to give evidence, the advocate representing the instructing party will question the expert first. This is known as the **examination-in-chief**. Its object is to elicit from the expert all the facts supporting the party's case. The examination-in-chief will usually begin with questions about the expert's qualifications and experience and the methodology used in preparing the report.

Experts must be open and unbiased, unlike lawyers!

The expert in court has a special responsibility to assist the court in coming to a just conclusion. Experts should not be partisan and should not seek to hide matters that help or hinder one party or the other. This role is in contrast to that of the lawyers, who are partisan and whose questions will be designed to present a client's case to its best advantage.

Consequently, expert witnesses should not be afraid to expand on a reply to a question and should not allow answers to be driven by the examining advocate. When in doubt, the expert should ask the judge for permission to offer a fuller explanation and, where necessary, to use visual aids and other materials if these will assist in presenting the evidence in a way that will be more easily understood.

Ask judge for permission to give fuller explanations to clarify

Questions phrased to obviously steer a witness towards giving a particular response (**leading questions**) should not be asked in an examination-in-chief except when there are uncontested facts and with the leave of the judge.

Leading questions generally not permitted from the instructing party

In expressing an opinion, the expert should take into consideration all the material facts before the court **at the time the opinion is expressed**. If, for any reason, the expert is not satisfied that the opinion can be expressed finally and without qualification, the expert should indicate that the opinion is provisional or qualified.

Must consider all material facts before the court at the time

Finally, experts should take great care to confine their responses and opinions to:

Confine response to matters material to dispute

- **matters material to the dispute** between the parties, and

- **matters that lie within their expertise**.

But it should be recognised that this 'knowledge boundary' is not always so clear cut. Accordingly, experts should make the court aware when a particular issue falls near the periphery of their area of expertise.

Inform court when issues approach limits of expertise

Cross-examination

Cross-examination after evidence-in-chief

After the conclusion of the examination-in-chief the other party (or parties) will have the opportunity to put its own questions to the expert witness. This is known as **cross-examination**. If the expert witness has said nothing to damage that party's case, or with which its own expert disagrees, there may be no need to cross-examine the expert at all. In that case the expert's evidence will generally be taken to be accepted by both parties.

Cross-examination may be hostile, so take care

Where cross-examination of experts takes place, it may or may not be hostile in nature. The expert may simply be asked to expand, or clarify, responses given in his examination-in-chief, or to state an opinion based on a slightly different hypothetical premise. However, the cross-examination may be an all-out attempt to discredit the expert's evidence. For example, an attack may focus on the expert's qualifications and credentials, scientific literature may be adduced containing authorities contradicting the evidence given or ridiculing the methodology used, etc.

Data, facts, tests, observations and truths will all be questioned

A cross-examiner will frequently question the validity of data, facts, tests, observations or truths generally accepted to be within the expert's field of expertise. An expert can be cross-examined about the bases of the opinion, regardless of whether those bases were canvassed under the examination-in-chief. The expert can also be asked to explain the significance of each step of the procedure followed.

Beware leading questions and 'yes' or 'no' answers

As the scope for cross-examining of experts is much wider than it is for ordinary witnesses, the advocate might also ask about materials not considered, tests not conducted and data not reviewed, as well as the implications of these. Bear in mind that in cross-examination it is permissible to ask leading questions, and the skilful advocate will often seek to take control by asking such questions or those that require a simple 'yes' or 'no' answer.

The techniques that the advocate employs are many and various. These will range from the aggressive to the flattering, and may well involve questions designed to unsettle or cause the expert to lose his temper or objective demeanour.

Techniques employed to unsettle – so stay calm

As Professor I H Dennis has said[1]

'... witnesses will not generally be questioned by anyone involved in the proceedings in a spirit of free impartial inquiry. Partisan, controlled questioning is the norm, and free report by the witness is the exception. This point helps to explain why some witnesses find the process of testifying at best bewildering, because they are unable to tell their story in their own way, or at worst traumatic, because of 'robust' cross-examination which may have the effect of making them feel that they themselves are on trial'.

Remember it's usually not personal

As unpleasant as it can be, cross-examination is seen as the most effective device:

Cross-examination is effective, if occasionally unpleasant

- to **test the veracity of witnesses**
- to **expose the dishonest, mistaken or unreliable**, and
- to **uncover inconsistencies and inaccuracies** in oral testimony.

By its very nature, cross-examination is designed to produce answers favourable to the cross-examiner and that cast doubt on the accuracy of the evidence given by the witness.

Questioning designed to give favourable answers

---

[1] *The Law of Evidence* [1999] Sweet & Maxwell, p 428.

The 'golden rules' for the expert are:

- **Maintain a measured and calm approach.**
- You are there to **assist the court** and it is to the court that you owe your primary duty.
- Although the barrister will ask the questions, **answers should be addressed to the judge.**
- **Take your time, be deliberate and make sure you fully understand the question** before giving your answer. If you do not understand a question, or if a question seems ambiguous, you should ask the advocate to repeat or clarify it.
- If the judge is taking notes, **watch the pen** and make sure he can keep up with the answers.
- Only answer the question asked and **be succinct.** Don't feel obliged to fill a silence!
- **Be vigilant for the ambiguous question** that could have a double meaning or assumes an answer not given to an earlier question.
- **Avoid vague expressions** like 'substantial', 'probable' and 'significant' as they are likely to be seized upon in cross-examination in an attempt to undermine the expert's credibility.
- For the same reason, if something can't be remembered, say so – **don't guess.**

An expert's demeanour when responding

When responding to cross-examination:

- **Do not be over-enthusiastic** and **do not exaggerate** as these can lead to suggestions of bias.
- **Do not be evasive or aggressive** and never lose your temper.
- **Maintain an objective approach** and acknowledge the existence of alternatives when it is reasonable to do so.

- **Do not be flippant.**
- **Never fence or argue** with the advocate.
- Try to **be courteous**, no matter how irritated you might become.
- Remember that **it's not personal!**

In the 1990s the Runciman Royal Commission was asked to consider unfairness to witnesses by the incompetence or overbearing behaviour of advocates and the failure, on occasion, of judges to control such conduct. Since then, much has been done by way of training and codes of conduct to improve the general quality of advocacy.

Judges are now more alert than formerly to their power and duty to intervene to prevent repetitious or otherwise unnecessary evidence and to control irrelevant or oppressive questioning of witnesses. It remains true that cross-examination can still be an ordeal to be endured. However, the traditional image of the expert being torn to shreds by skilful cross-examination is actually quite rare. Experts should bear in mind that, in reality, advocates are often at a disadvantage in that they do not possess sufficient in-depth knowledge of the specific field of expertise to enable them to effectively cross-examine the witness.

Judges now very aware of powers to protect expert from badgering

Length of cross-examination

The court has the power to regulate or limit the length of time a party will be permitted to cross-examine a witness (see *BCCI -v- The Bank of England*)[2]. The court has held that under normal circumstances 28 days should be more than ample time and, in serious cases of high public interest, 40 days should be the maximum. The test to be

Court can limit the duration of cross-examination

---

[2] *BCCI -v- The Bank of England* [2005] *EWCA Civ* 889.

imposed by the trial judge is: 'How long is it necessary for the cross-examination to last in the interests of justice, the parties and the witness?' Of course, the BCCI case involved lay witnesses, and it is possible that the court might consider longer time limits for the cross-examination of experts as witnesses.

Re-examination

Judge can ask questions to clarify or explore further areas

During the examination-in-chief or cross-examination, the judge might put questions to the expert. These will usually be designed to clarify an answer given or to explore an area the judge considers particularly significant.

Jury can ask questions in writing

In those very rare circumstances in which a jury is hearing the case, it can also put questions to the expert. These will be in the form of a written request to the judge.

Re-examination permitted to clarify only

After cross-examination has concluded, the party that originally called the expert witness may conduct a re-examination of that witness. However, the party must limit questions to clarify only those matters that arose during cross-examination. Leading questions may not be asked.

Rarely a party can recall a witness after it has closed its case

Re-examination of a witness is not always carried out. It can be tactically disadvantageous and could serve only to make a bad situation worse. In some circumstances the court itself can recall a witness for further examination or cross-examination. Indeed, in rare cases a party might be permitted to call evidence after it has closed its case to rebut evidence that was totally unforeseen.

General advice

General rules of good conduct

By way of conclusion we offer these general words of advice:

- Do not dress as if for a job interview. You should aim for the **smart professional look** but wear what you feel comfortable in.

- **Arrive at court in good time**. On arrival, consult the court list which will be posted on the notice board in the court foyer. Note the court you are in. Then locate your instructing advocate or the court usher. If in doubt about what you should do, the volunteers who staff the Witness Service can be very helpful.

- **Take a note of the trial or case number**. This will help you identify the case at a later date and may be needed when you claim your fee or expenses.

- **Expect to have your bags checked** at the entrance to the court building and do not take anything with you that is likely to cause a problem.

- Remember to **switch off your mobile phone** before entering the courtroom.

- **Make sure you are well prepared** and have everything you are likely to need.

- As an expert witness you will usually be permitted to **sit in court and listen** to the preceding evidence in the case. However, make sure you ask permission first as this will be at the discretion of the court.

- When giving your evidence **direct your remarks directly to the jury or**, if there is no jury, **to the judge**.

- Bear in mind that, even when the proceedings are being tape recorded, the judge will usually wish to take notes. Accordingly, **do not rush your evidence**; it helps to watch the judge's pen.

Observe rules and etiquette and you'll be treated fairly

A first court appearance can be confusing and sometimes intimidating. It is certainly not for the feint of heart. Even the experienced witness can find procedural matters bewildering at times. However, by correctly observing rules of conduct and court etiquette the expert's path will be made somewhat easier.

7 Payment of Fees

This is, without doubt, the thorniest issue of all, and indeed a volume in this series is dedicated to examining chapter and verse on the topic – *The Little Book on Expert Fees*.[1] It's a subject on which each expert must make up his own mind, especially considering the commercial implications of any one approach. What follows here is merely an introduction to the subject, more details of which can be gained by reading the aforementioned title.

For more detailed analysis order The Little Book on Expert Fees

A matter of contract

The relationship between an expert witness and the instructing solicitor is a contractual one, whether or not it has been reduced to writing. It follows that if, for example, they have agreed the fee the expert is to be paid (or the basis on which it is to be calculated) and the timing of its payment, the solicitor is **personally responsible for paying that fee in full and within that time span**. This is so even if:

Lawyer personally responsible for expert's fee

- the solicitor has not at that stage been paid by the client (or whoever else is funding the litigation), or

---

[1] See *www.jspubs.com/LittleBooks* for further details.

- the solicitor should eventually receive less than the full amount from one or other of them.

If no contract in place, then if fee reasonable the lawyer should pay within reasonable time

If, as happens all too often, the expert fails to stipulate a fee or neglects to mention how soon payment is required, then, subject to other relevant factors (such as whether the fees claimed are reasonable with regard to the work done), the solicitor should pay the amount stated in the expert's bill within a reasonable time.

No implied term that expert will accept less after assessment

There is no implied term here that the expert witness will be prepared to accept either what is allowed on assessment of the costs of the case or on assessment of his fees by the Legal Services Commission. Nor can the expert be deemed ready to wait for settlement of the bill until (say) the solicitor has received a payment from the latter.

Solicitor must disclaim personal responsibility at outset to avoid contractual obligation

Only if the solicitor has expressly disclaimed personal responsibility for payment of fees beyond what is allowed or assessed, or until he is in funds, can the solicitor evade the contractual obligation to the expert. Unless the solicitor has made this disclaimer, it follows too that if an expert's fee, or the full amount of it, is not allowed on assessment of the costs of the case, the solicitor must bear the deficit.

Naturally enough, solicitors do not like to be left in this situation, any more than experts like working on the basis that they will accept being paid whatever a court or a legal aid official may decide. Fortunately, it is not a situation that is likely to arise very often in privately funded civil cases, and in publicly funded ones well-oiled procedures exist which go a long way towards eliminating the risks for either party.

Solicitor's personal liability

A solicitor is personally liable for paying the 'proper costs' (i.e. fees and disbursements) of any expert instructed on behalf of a client. Moreover, this is so whether or not the solicitor has been placed in funds by the client, the client's insurers or the Legal Services Commission.

Personal liability whether or not in funds

The only ways in which a solicitor may legitimately escape these responsibilities towards the expert are:

Ways for lawyer to escape responsibility for fees

- if an agreement has been made to the contrary

- if the solicitor has expressly disclaimed these responsibilities in his letter of instruction (in which case, of course, the expert could decline to be instructed), or

- if the expert has declined an invitation to give his evidence in court and has had to be served with a witness summons.[2]

This, however, largely ignores the reality of the situation in which experts usually find themselves in their dealings with solicitors – it is solicitors who normally call the tune. Hence the growing frequency with which experts are being asked to agree to their invoices being paid much later than they would like or normally expect. Indeed, in some reported instances experts have received payment as much as 2 years after invoices have been presented. It is very much a matter of business judgment on the part of the expert as to whether he can afford to comply with such requests.

Lawyers usually call the shots and payment is delayed

---

[2] For further details of what this entails, see *Chapter 8: The Witness Summons.*

Contingency fees

Never make fees contingent on outcome of case

A still more serious phenomenon, because it raises ethical considerations as well, are the requests sometimes made of experts that they accept part payment of their fee on presentation of their invoice but waive the balance in the event of the client losing the case. This quite definitely makes payment of the expert contingent on the outcome of the litigation and is not permitted by the rules of court. If this arrangement ever came to light it would immediately bring into question the expert's independence and objectivity. Never, ever, incur that risk.

Dealing with delayed payment

27% of experts claim solicitors always delay payment

Whatever arrangement may have been agreed for the payment of fees, the most common experience of all is that payment will be delayed – sometimes inordinately so. A survey undertaken by the *UK Register of Expert Witnesses* in June 2005 revealed that only 45% of the experts who took part in it were able to report that their instructing solicitors paid up on time in even the majority of instances, while 27% claimed that solicitors never did so.

Options for chasing payment

An expert faced with this situation has a limited number of options.

* A **periodic reminder** to the solicitor or the firm's accounts department.

Highlight professional responsibility

* A **letter to the firm's senior partner**. The expert might, for example, choose to remind the partner of the obligation laid on solicitors by the Law Society's *Guide to the Professional Conduct of Solicitors*, i.e. that solicitors should pay the proper costs of any professional agent they instruct on behalf of a client, whether or not they have themselves

been paid by the client, and to do so within a reasonable time.

The Law Society of England and Wales's *Guide to the Professional Conduct of Solicitors* states the matter as follows:

'Principle 20.01: Duty to pay agents' fees. A solicitor is personally responsible for paying the proper costs of any professional agent or other person whom he or she instructs on behalf of a client, whether or not the solicitor receives payment from the client, unless the solicitor and the person instructed make an express agreement to the contrary'.

- **Lodge a complaint** about the solicitor's tardiness with the *Consumer Complaints Service* (CCS) of the Law Society[3]. However, under procedures that took effect in June 1999, the CCS will take action only when the complainant can produce evidence of a court judgment against the solicitor in respect of which no appeal is outstanding.

  Complain to Consumer Complaints Service

- **Sue for the money.**[4] It is a matter for individual judgment whether the amount owed is large enough, or the solicitor's behaviour sufficiently flagrant, to justify the cost and risks involved in taking that step. If the claim is for less than £5,000 it ought to be possible to use the small claims procedure to recover the debt. A mere threat to do so may be all that is needed to secure payment. It is pretty certain,

  Sue as a small claim if bill less than £5,000

---

[3] The Consumer Complaint's Service of the Law Society can be contacted on 0845 608 6565.

[4] Readers minded to use the small claims procedure to recover debts owed to them by clients, solicitors included, may like to know that the Courts Service has published a series of leaflets detailing the steps that need to be taken. Copies may be obtained from any county court.

though, that once voiced, such a threat would result in no more instructions being received from the firm concerned.

Single joint experts

Joint and several liability for payment

CPR 35.8(3) provides that the court may give instructions about the payment of an SJE's fees and expenses, but it does not have to do so. If it does not, the SJE could well experience difficulty in securing payment for his services, notwithstanding the fact that the instructing parties will normally be jointly and severally liable in that respect.

It is, of course, a fact of life that solicitors may be slow in paying the experts they instruct on behalf of their clients. But where an SJE has to invoice each party separately, the situation can be even worse. In those circumstances the solicitor acting for the losing party may be even less inclined to settle promptly, especially if he had not wished to see an SJE appointed in the first place.

Aim for just one paymaster

The obvious solution to this particular problem is to have just one paymaster. Experts invited to act as an SJE would be well advised to make that a condition of their acceptance of joint appointment. Although it still does not follow that they will be paid promptly, it should at least cut down the amount of payment chasing they have to do.

In the long run, of course, it is likely that one of the parties will end up meeting the entire cost of an expert jointly appointed by them both.

Ensure contract includes term stipulating fees not subject to assessment

Another point to bear in mind, though, is that in making any order as to the costs of the case, the court might still disallow some of those incurred for expert evidence, even though it has been provided by an SJE. For this reason, it would be as well for experts who are asked to accept a joint appointment to secure the written agreement of both parties to their normal terms of engagement, included among which should be a clause stipulating that fees and expenses are not subject to assessment but must be paid **in full**.

Note, too, that should the court direct that the parties to a case appoint an SJE to provide evidence on a particular issue, it also has the power to limit in advance the amount the expert is to be paid. Any expert invited to act as an SJE in those circumstances will need to consider very carefully whether the assignment is such that he can afford to accept the appointment. At the very least, the expert will have to monitor most carefully the time expended on the case, since over-running the budget set by the court could result in the expert being seriously out of pocket by the end of the case.

Court can limit expert fee in advance

8 The Witness Summons

Oral testimony is one of the bastions of our adversarial system of justice. In civil litigation, it is true, the Woolf reforms have restricted its use to some extent. But even here it remains important that parties should be able to call witnesses to testify in court and, if necessary, compel them to do so. A **summons** is the means provided to ensure attendance of the witness.

A summons compels court attendance

In civil cases, a further use of the witness summons is to secure:

It can also secure production of documents

- the **production of documents** for the court, and

- the attendance at a preliminary hearing of **witnesses who can attest to the authenticity** of the documents.

This may be particularly necessary if the documents are held by a non-party and one of the litigants wishes to have sight of them before trial of the action.[1]

Civil procedure

In the High Court, the witness summons used to be known – indeed, for more than five centuries was

Consequence of non-compliance dire

---

[1] For example, at a so-called Khanna hearing (see *Khanna -v- Lovell White Durrant* [1995] *1 WLR* 121).

known – as a *subpoena* (from the Latin: *sub*, under; *poena*, penalty), which neatly indicated the likely consequence of non-compliance. Alas, that evocative Latinism was one of many swept away by the Woolf reforms. What we have in its place is the purely descriptive term that has been employed all along by the county courts. The change does serve to emphasise, though, that for all civil courts in England and Wales the rules governing the procedure are now the same – as, indeed, are the forms used when applying for and issuing a summons.

Who may be summoned, and how?

Competent witnesses can be compelled to attend court

In principle, any witness who is considered competent to give evidence in a civil case can be compelled to attend court for that purpose. A witness is 'competent' if it is lawful for him to give evidence, and that is a matter for the judge to decide. The expert is 'compellable' if it is lawful to oblige him to give evidence, and that is governed by statute.[2]

Experts must also be competent in their discipline

The competence of witnesses of fact is generally a question of whether they have sufficient understanding of the importance of the proceedings for their evidence to be heard. In the case of expert witnesses, it also involves competence in a discipline relevant to the matters in issue.

Summons must be issued by court holding hearing

A summons requiring the attendance of a witness can only be issued by the court where the case is proceeding or the hearing in question is to be held.

The summons has to be applied for by the party needing the witness's evidence. Generally speaking its issue will be automatic. The court's permission is required only if:

---

[2] Principally the various Acts conferring sovereign or diplomatic immunity.

- **the witness is wanted for a hearing other than the trial** of the action, or

- **the trial itself is due to start in less than 7 days.**

Fortunately, for those on the receiving end of a summons, there is a further safeguard built into the procedure (see page 155). This is that a court may, in the exercise of its discretion, set aside a summons issued previously if it can be persuaded that the summons was not sought in good faith or was oppressive in its effect. It could be, for example, that there are a number of witnesses equally competent to provide the evidence required, and the expert who has actually been summoned can make out a good case for not appearing, such as unreasonable disruption of his work.

Court can set aside summons if not sought in good faith

This affords an important protection to experts – and especially, perhaps, for the better known – for they might otherwise receive all manner of speculative summonses to give evidence in cases with which they have had no prior involvement. As Mr Justice Cooke observed in a case decided in 1973, 'the English courts will not as a general rule require an expert to give expert evidence against his wishes in a case where he has had no connection with the facts or the history of the matter in issue'.[3]

Court offers protection for well known experts

Why summon an expert?

The two legitimate reasons why litigants might wish to have an expert summoned are:

- they know, or believe, that **the expert is unwilling to give evidence in court** or produce the required documents, or

---
[3] *Seyfang -v- Searle & Co* [1973] *1 QB* 148.

- there is a risk **the expert may be prevented from doing so**.

Reasons to decline court appearance

It is unusual for an expert to decline to give oral evidence in a case for which instructions have been received previously, but it does happen from time to time and for a variety of reasons.

- It may be that the instructing solicitor has been slow in paying for the report commissioned and **the expert is trying to exert pressure to settle the invoice**. As we shall see, this is a tactic that can seriously backfire.

- Another reason might be that **the client has indicated he is no longer able to pay the expert's fee** for giving evidence in court. Here it is the litigant who is on weaker ground and the summons may well be set aside.

- Then again, it may be that **the expert is reluctant to give evidence** simply because it is being sought by the opponents of the party that first instructed him.

There is no property in an expert witness

Lord Denning's famous ruling, that 'there is no property in a witness', was designed to put an expert in much the same position as a witness of fact.[4] It was considered that, while communications between lawyers and experts are privileged, the court was entitled to have the facts the expert had seen adduced in evidence. Denning took the view that to allow such evidence to be excluded on grounds of privilege, or on the basis that there was a contract between the expert and the instructing party, would be contrary to public policy.

---

[4] *Harmony Shipping Co SA -v- Saudi Europe Line Ltd* [1979] *1 WLR* 1380.

However, the compellability of expert witnesses in both civil and criminal proceedings is now subject to common law exceptions in cases involving experts who have previously been instructed by one party or another. The courts have now ruled that an opinion can be privileged in circumstances where it is based on privileged material. Such material can be in the form of documents or merely conversations between the party and the expert.[5]

Exceptions if opinion based on privileged material

For example, in *R -v- Rahman*, the accused's solicitors had instructed a fingerprint expert who gave them his opinion and a report. The expert was not called to give evidence by the defence, but in the course of the trial he sat behind the defendant's barrister and advised him during cross-examination of the prosecution's witnesses.

Observing this, prosecuting counsel applied to the judge for permission to call the expert himself. The defence objected, claiming that both the opinion they had received from him and the advice he was giving in court were privileged. If he were to be called by the prosecution, that privilege would be broken and the defendant exposed to the risk of self-incrimination.

However, defending counsel also argued that if such a tactic were to be allowed, defence solicitors everywhere would be inhibited from instructing experts for fear they might produce adverse reports. If they did do so, and the prosecution suspected as much, it could then take advantage of the situation to the detriment of the accused, thereby denying a fair trial as envisaged in Articles 5 and 6 of the European Convention on Human Rights (ECHR). The judge agreed and refused leave to call the expert.

---

[5] *R -v- Rahman* unreported; *R -v- Davies* [2002] *WLR* 1806.

Securing release from other duties

A summons secures release from other duties

The other reason for summoning an expert is altogether much more common. It could be that the expert, though perfectly willing to give evidence, needs a summons to secure release from other duties – as happens, for example, when a police expert is required to testify on a civil matter. A still more frequent occurrence is that the expert is working on two cases that are due to go to trial at the same time, and a clash of dates is feared.

In the past, if that materialised, the solicitors concerned would have reckoned on coming to an amicable agreement whereby one of them applied for a postponement of the client's hearing to enable the expert to give evidence in both cases. In such circumstances, too, courts almost invariably agreed to one. Under the CPR regime of case management, however, an application of that sort is nowadays much less likely to succeed. In current circumstances, issuing a witness summons may be the only means by which a solicitor can secure priority over the expert's services for the client's benefit.

Practicalities

See CPR Part 34 for detailed rules

The rules governing the issue of witness summonses are contained in Part 34 of the CPR and may be summarised as follows:

- A witness summons is a document (Form N20) issued by a court on application from one of the parties to an action or their solicitors.

- No permission is required of the court to issue the summons – unless, that is, the trial is taking place in less than 7 days or attendance is being sought on a date other than that of the trial or for a hearing other than the trial.

- A court may issue a summons for proceedings before an inferior court or tribunal that lacks the power to issue one itself.

- The summons is binding on the recipient providing it is served at least 7 days before the date on which attendance is first required (although the court may waive that condition). It remains in force for the duration of the trial or hearing, or until the judge decides that the witness is no longer needed.

  Summons binding if served at least 7 days before date required

- The summons will be served by the court unless the party on whose behalf it is issued states in writing that he wishes to serve it.

- At the time of service, the witness must be offered or paid an amount to cover travelling expenses and compensation for loss of time (which sum must be stated on the summons).

  Must be offered travel expenses and compensation at time of service

- If the court is serving the summons, the party on whose behalf it is being issued must deposit this sum at the court office.

As can be seen, most of this is quite straightforward. It does, however, beg a number of questions of particular significance for experts, namely:

- How is a summons served?
- What kind of payment is due?
- In what circumstances can a summons be set aside?
- What are the consequences of non-compliance?

Service

If the court is effecting service, it will normally send the summons by first-class post. Whether or not this

Service usually by first-class post

is appropriate will depend on the circumstances. If the witness is being summoned for 'friendly' reasons, e.g. to enable other commitments to be broken, service by post should be quite sufficient – providing, of course, it is done far enough in advance to ensure that the witness has the required notice of 7 days.

For unwilling witnesses, service by process server

If, on the other hand, the witness is believed to be unwilling to give evidence or to produce the documents sought, the solicitor initiating the procedure may elect to have the summons delivered by a process server. This will have the aim of impressing upon the witness:

* the **importance of complying** with the summons and
* the potentially **serious consequences** of not doing so.

Payment must be offered at time of service

In these circumstances, the process server must also tender the necessary payment. If it is not offered or paid at the time of service, the witness would be able to apply to the issuing court for the summons to be set aside.

Payment

Experts can claim travel expenses and compensation

As the above summary of the Rules indicates, there are two elements in the payment that witnesses are entitled to receive:

* their **travelling expenses** – a sum 'reasonably sufficient' to cover the cost of getting to and from the court, and
* **compensation** for their loss of time.

The total payment is known as **conduct money**.

When a solicitor causes a witness summons to be issued in a civil case, it is the solicitor, not the court, who remunerates the witness.

Willing expert witnesses

If the summons is to be served on an expert who is happy to attend court, but who needs the summons to escape an obligation to be elsewhere, the Law Society's *Guide to the Professional Conduct of Solicitors* stipulates that the solicitor should pay the expert whatever was agreed previously between them for the latter's appearance in court. Indeed, the use of the witness summons to try to avoid paying the willing expert will fail – as the case of *Brown -v-Bennett* shows.[6]

Compensation based on court attendance fees already stipulated

Unwilling expert witnesses

The solicitor is not obliged to do that, though, if the witness has declined to give evidence for any reason. In this event, the solicitor need observe only the DCA's guidelines in fixing the amount to be offered. Of course, if the solicitor's offer should be less than the minimum specified by the DCA, the expert could apply to the court to have the summons set aside. Otherwise the expert has little option but to accept the payment. Refusing to do so does not excuse the expert from obeying the summons.

Unwilling experts need be offered payment according to DCA guidelines only

DCA guidance

Rule 34.7(b) defines the compensation element of the conduct money as 'such sum by way of compensation... for loss of time as may be specified in the relevant practice direction'. On consulting the Practice Direction to Part 34, one finds that it is 'to be based on the sums payable to witnesses attending the Crown Court'.

DCA guidance based on Crown Court attendance allowance

As any expert who has given evidence in a Crown Court will know, attendance allowances there are paid according to rates and scales fixed by the DCA

---

[6] *Brown & Brown -v- Bennett & Others* [2000] *TLR* 2 November.

(the Lord Chancellor's Department as was). In the case of 'ordinary' witnesses, maximum amounts are specified, depending on the period of their absence from work.

Scales allow determining officers to assess claims

As there are no prescribed scales for the allowance for remuneration of expert witnesses and certain other persons such as interpreters, the DCA has issued guidelines to assist determining officers. These guidelines are designed to provide a point of reference on quantum for use by determining officers when exercising their discretion in determining claims. They can also be of use to those making claims when determining their entitlements. The figures shown in Table 1 (see page 155) are based on allowances made throughout England and Wales and are correct as at May 2003. It was intended by the DCA that the figures should be revised annually – which, of course, they never are!

Consider work done, status of expert and local availability of expertise

In exercising their discretion, determining officers are to bear in mind that each case must be considered individually. They are to take into account all the relevant circumstances surrounding the claim, including such things as the work done, the status or experience of the person doing the work, and the availability of such persons in the area of the country concerned.

Allowances meagre in comparison with usual fee

Only in exceptional circumstances would the courts pay more. Indeed, it should come as no surprise to anyone that even the maxima on these guidance scales are way below the fees most experts would expect to charge for a day in court if they were free to negotiate them.

Conclusion

Unwilling expert witnesses risk poor payment

It will be abundantly clear, then, that an expert witness should think long and hard about the consequences of becoming an unwilling expert witness.

Table1: Schedule of Rates from 6 May 2003

1. *Consultant medical practitioner, psychiatrist, pathologist*
    Preparation (examination/report):   £70–£100 per hour
    Attendance at court (full day):   £346–£500

2. *Fire (assessor) and/or explosives expert*
    Preparation: £50–£75 per hour
    Attendance at court (full day):   £255–£365

3. *Forensic scientist (including questioned document
    examiner), surveyor, accountant, engineer, medical
    practitioner, architect, veterinary surgeon, meteorologist*
    Preparation: £47–£100 per hour
    Attendance at court (full day):   £226–£490

4. *Fingerprint [expert]*
    Preparation: £32–£52 per hour
    Attendance at court (full day):   £153–£256

5. *Interpreter* (with a minimum of 3 hours for those employed
    regularly in this capacity)
    £25–£28 (per hour)

Setting a summons aside

As we have seen, a court has the power to set aside any witness summons it has issued previously. This may be done for any of a number of reasons.

Court can rescind a summons

An application to have a summons set aside is made to the procedural judge in charge of the case. The judge's concern will be to determine whether the party that requested issue abused its privilege in summoning the witness. The summons will be set aside:

Apply to procedural judge in charge of case

- if, for example, it appears to the judge that the **request was speculative** and the party making it was merely fishing for evidence

Did requesting party abuse the process?

- if the judge was satisfied that the witness who had been summoned **had no evidence to give of relevance** to the case or, if an expert

155

witness, 'when he has no connection with the facts or the history of the matter'.[7]

- if those serving the summons had **failed to meet the CPR requirements** concerning payment to the witness
- if, in the case of an expert, it should appear to the court that issue of the summons had been sought to **avoid having to pay the expert** a previously agreed fee – as happened in the case of *Brown and Brown -v- Bennett and others.*[8]

Avoid paying expert

The claimants, Graham and Edwina Brown, were shareholders and directors in a company that went into liquidation. They alleged various kinds of wrongdoing by no fewer than 12 defendants – six of whom were also former directors of the company – and were claiming substantial damages. The issues raised by the case need not concern us here, but they were complicated. The trial of the action was expected to last several weeks.

Claimants attempted summons to avoid paying expert

Until a very late stage the Browns had the benefit of legal aid, and this met the cost of the reports from their two expert witnesses, one of whom was Tracey Callaghan, an insolvency specialist with Baker Tilly. Then legal aid was withdrawn and the Browns told Ms Callaghan that they were no longer able to pay her fee for attending court to give evidence at the trial of their action. She responded that in that case she was not prepared to show up, whereupon the Browns made an ex parte application for her to be summoned to do so.

---

[7] *Lively -v- City of Munich* [1976] *3 AER* 85, per Kerr J, citing the Seyfang case.

[8] *Brown & Brown -v- Bennett & Others* [2000] *TLR* 2 November.

At a hearing before Mr Justice Neuberger, counsel for Ms Callaghan successfully argued that when a litigant agreed to pay an expert witness a fee for giving evidence, he should not be allowed to resort to the procedural device of a witness summons to escape paying that fee. Were he to attempt this, the summons should be set aside, almost as a matter of course.

His Lordship agreed and duly released Ms Callaghan from observance of the summons, citing in support of his decision a passage from *Phipson on Evidence*, the standard textbook on the subject. As it happened, the Browns might not have needed Ms Callaghan's presence in court anyway, because during the hearing counsel for the defendants indicated that they were prepared to accept the evidence of her report as it stood.

Such considerations were, however, soon rendered immaterial, for a few days later the same judge accepted submissions on behalf of the defendants that the evidence so far disclosed revealed no adequate cause for action. He thereupon dismissed all claims against them.

Nothing to say

What is equally clear, though, is that a witness served with a summons cannot have it set aside merely by swearing that he can give no material evidence. Moreover, if it is an expert who is making the application, the judge hearing it may refuse to do as asked on the grounds that important factual information may be lost to the court should the expert not give evidence.

As Lord Justice Dunn observed in a criminal case decided in 1983, 'the court is entitled, in order to ascertain the truth, to have the actual facts which the expert has observed adduced before it'[9]. He cited in support of this Lord Denning's judgment in a civil case 10 years previously[10]. It is implicit, too, in the CPR, both:

- in meeting their overriding objective of enabling **courts to deal with cases justly**, and
- in respect of the duty the Rules lay on **experts to help the court on matters within their expertise**.

Penalties

Penalties for non-compliance include fine and/or imprisonment

Strangely enough, there is no reference in Part 34 of the Rules to the penalties for non-compliance with a witness summons. However, provisions of the former rules of court that have been re-enacted as schedules to the CPR make the defaulter liable:

- **to imprisonment for contempt of court** if the summons was issued in the High Court, or
- **to a fine** if it was issued by a county court.

In addition, the expert may be ordered to pay the costs resulting from failure to attend court. Draconian punishment, indeed, that no one in their right mind should lightly risk incurring.

---

[9] *R -v- King* [1983] *1 WLR* 411.

[10] *Seyfang -v- Searle & Co* [1973] *1 QB* 148.

9 Immunity

As a matter of public policy, all witnesses in legal proceedings, including expert witnesses, are immune from claims for damages resulting from anything said or done in court. Expert witnesses are no exception to this rule.

However, this does not mean that an expert is immune from any action arising out of his conduct as an expert witness. If he commits perjury he could face criminal proceedings. If he brings his profession into disrepute he may face professional disciplinary proceedings. And if his actions waste court time, he may even end up paying some of the costs in the case. So, how much immunity does an expert witness actually enjoy?

Immunity from civil suit

It is a well-established rule of law that anyone involved directly in legal proceedings – whether as judge, member of the jury, advocate or witness – is absolutely immune from civil action for anything he may say or do in court. If witnesses were to lie while under oath, they would, of course, risk being prosecuted for perjury. But that is a criminal offence, not a civil one. What is quite clear is that **experts cannot be sued for libel, malicious falsehood,**

negligence or even for conspiring to give false evidence.

Absolute immunity to encourage freedom of expression

The policy justification for this absolute immunity is not to provide a benefit to the individual, but to help the courts reach just decisions by encouraging all who take part in court proceedings to express themselves freely. With regard to witnesses, it was given classic expression by Lord Justice Salmon in *Marrinan -v- Vibart*[1], a House of Lords appeal decided in the early 1960s:

Expert immunity exists for benefit of the public

'This immunity exists for the benefit of the public, since the administration of justice would be greatly impeded if witnesses were to be in fear that any disgruntled and possibly impecunious persons against whom they gave evidence might subsequently involve them in costly litigation.'

And that statement applies as much today as it did then.

Duty to court overrides duty to instructing party

With **expert witnesses**, of course, there is a further consideration: namely that in preparing or giving their evidence they owe a duty to the court which overrides any obligation they have to those instructing them or by whom they are paid.[2] Consequently, experts may need protection from their instructing party as much as from anyone against whom they give evidence.

Widening scope of immunity

Concept of immunity derives from case law

The concept of immunity derives from case law: it is not statute based. It is important to bear this in mind

---

[1] *Marrinan -v- Vibart* [1963] *3 AER* 380.

[2] Although long established in case law, this overriding duty to the court has now been given statutory force by virtue of CPR 35.3(2).

when considering the evolution of immunity and recent developments affecting it. Just as immunity has been developed by judges, it is equally capable of being modified by them.

One way in which the concept has changed over the years has been in the extension of the protection immunity affords to cover things said or done before trial. Thus, in the *Marrinan* case cited earlier, the Court of Appeal held that immunity protected witnesses:

Immunity extended to include pre-trial preparations

* in the **preparation of their evidence**, as well as

* for any **evidence they gave in court**.

If this was not so, the protection they enjoyed while in the witness box could be outflanked by suing them for statements made in proofs of evidence taken beforehand.

For exactly the same reason, immunity attaches to any report an expert witness may be instructed to prepare, whether for civil or criminal proceedings. Moreover, the immunity applies even when, as is fast becoming general practice in civil proceedings, the expert is not called to give evidence in court and the report is all the evidence provided.

Immunity also attaches to expert reports

Expert advisor

It will be apparent from the foregoing that claims for damages against expert witnesses in respect of evidence they give in court, or are instructed to prepare for use in court, are doomed to failure. What, though, of those other services experts provide in civil disputes? They are often asked, for example:

Beware the role of expert advisor

* to investigate the circumstances that gave rise to the dispute

- to conduct experiments to determine their cause
- to advise on the strengths and weaknesses of the client's case
- to identify technical weaknesses in the opposing side's expert evidence
- to assist in negotiations to settle the dispute.

Immunity uncertain as experts stray towards role of advisor

The further the expert is away from the court the less certain the immunity becomes. So, in all these additional roles an expert may be called upon to perform, he is probably as liable to be sued for negligence as any other professional advisor. Moreover, this is likely to be so even if it was anticipated at the time the service was provided that the expert would be a witness in court should the matter proceed to trial.

Case law underpinning immunity from civil suit

As said previously, the concept of immunity is not statute based, but derives from case law. The leading case on the question of expert witness immunity is undoubtedly *Stanton -v- Callaghan*, decided by the Court of Appeal in July 1998.[3]

The case concerned a property that had suffered subsidence damage. Partial underpinning had been carried out, but this was not successful and further subsidence occurred. The defendant, a civil and structural engineer, was engaged by the owners to report on the problem, and he advised that the partial underpinning had been inappropriate. To restore the property to its full market value, total underpinning of the building would be required. On the strength of this advice, the owners made a claim under their buildings policy. When this was rejected, they

---

[3] *Stanton -v- Callaghan* [1998] *4 AER* 961.

initiated proceedings against the insurers. The engineer was to be their sole expert witness in the ensuing litigation.

At a preliminary hearing, directions were given that expert evidence should be agreed if at all possible, and the expert witnesses for both sides duly met to discuss possible remedies. At the meeting, the engineer, departing from the advice he had previously given his clients, agreed with the insurer's expert that the existing partial underpinning could be restructured at much less cost. He then produced a final report just a few days before the case came to trial in which he provided costings for both options and asserted that either of them would restore stability and return the property to its full market value, which was by now reckoned to be £105,000.

Expert changed opinion after meeting of experts

Not surprisingly, the agreement reached by the experts had an immediate impact on the value of the owners's claim, so much so that when the insurance company paid £16,000 into court, they felt constrained to accept this sum. On subsequently putting the property up for sale, however, the most they could get for it was £50,000.

The owners then sued the surveyor and his firm for the difference between the full market value had it been repaired and the amount they had been able to sell it for, with due allowance being made for the sum recovered from the insurers. They contended that his initial advice to them had been correct, and the basis of their claim was that he had been negligent and in breach of duty to them in:

Expert sued for negligence

(i) failing to inform them that he had substantially changed his mind as to possible remedies, and

(ii) allowing himself to be unduly influenced into changing his mind by the other expert's assertion that full underpinning represented a degree of betterment outside the terms of the owners's insurance policy.

At two previous hearings the engineer's lawyers had applied to have the action struck out on the ground that, as a prospective witness, he was immune from suit in respect of any report on which his evidence would be based or any agreement summarising evidence he would have given at trial. In both instances, though, the application was refused, with the judge in the second of them ruling that it was at least arguable that the expert ought to have told his clients what he was intending to do before entering into an agreement which, in effect, abandoned a large part of their case.

In the Court of Appeal, Lord Justice Chadwick identified the following propositions as supported by arguments binding on that court:

Court of Appeal confirms immunity in court and of report

'(i) an expert witness who gives evidence at a trial is immune from suit in respect of anything he says in court, and that immunity will extend to the content of the report he adopts as, or incorporates in, his evidence;

(ii) where an expert gives evidence at a trial the immunity which he would enjoy in respect of that evidence is not to be circumscribed by a suit based on the report itself;

Expert advisor not immune

(iii) the immunity does not extend to protect an expert who has been retained to advise as to the merits of a party's claim in litigation... notwithstanding that it was in contemplation when the advice was given that the expert would be a witness at the trial if that litigation were to proceed.'

The novel issue the Court of Appeal had to decide was whether an expert is immune in respect of the contents of a report he prepared for the purpose of court proceedings when in fact he did *not* give evidence at trial – either because the trial did not take place or he was not called as a witness.

Is expert immune if evidence not given?

In the event, the three judges hearing the case were unanimous that an expert would be immune in these circumstances, although they reached that decision by somewhat different routes, depending on what they took to be the predominant ground of public policy.

The answer is 'Yes!'

For Lord Justice Chadwick, it was:

Immunity covers changes of opinion following expert meetings

- the need for trials to take no longer than was necessary to do justice, and

- the consequent importance of encouraging experts to identify those parts of their evidence on which they were, and those on which they were not, in agreement.

If a court requires experts to meet for this purpose, they should be free to make proper concessions without fear that any departure from advice previously given would lay them open to being sued in negligence.

Lord Justice Orton, on the other hand, was not so sure that all experts might be equally immune in this respect. He drew a distinction between those who work for large professional firms, which have clauses in their terms of engagement designed to restrict or exclude liability for negligent advice, and others who, as in this case, act in an individual capacity without that degree of protection. On this point, though, his remarks are strictly *obiter*. It remains to be seen whether disgruntled clients of firms providing litigation support seek to develop arguments along these lines in future.

Expert immunity reaffirmed

In general, however, the Court of Appeal's decision in *Stanton -v- Callaghan* was good news for experts. It usefully reaffirmed the immune status of expert reports which '*can be fairly said to be preliminary to giving evidence in court*', even in circumstances where the experts are not called upon to give oral evidence. It also established that expert witnesses are immune from suit in respect of any agreements they may reach at meetings of experts ordered by the court.

Pressures on expert immunity

Unfortunately, though, this new-found certainty was all too soon dispelled by major developments on other fronts, namely:

- the introduction of the new CPR
- the coming into force of the Human Rights Act 1998, and
- the abandonment of advocate immunity.

Civil Procedure Rules

Does immunity extend to work in accordance with pre-action protocols?

There is plenty of scope for uncertainty over the extent of immunity under the CPR. Can it be said, for example, that experts are entitled to immunity in respect of reports exchanged in accordance with pre-action protocols?

The observance of such protocols is an essential element of the reforms the Rules were designed to bring about. Indeed, the Practice Direction concerning them states that in a dispute not specifically covered by an approved protocol, the parties should nevertheless conduct themselves as if covered by one – all with a view to settling the dispute before commencement of proceedings.

This leads to the anomalous situation that if the parties fail in their attempt to avoid issuing proceedings and rely on their expert reports in the ensuing litigation, the authors of the reports would become immune from suit. However, if they succeed in settling their dispute, the experts could be denied that protection, since no court would have become involved and the experts might be reckoned to have no other status than that of advisors. Moreover, for reasons explained below, it is now even more doubtful whether immunity could be claimed by an expert who has been *jointly* selected by the parties in pursuance of a pre-action protocol.

Experts working pre-action may not be immune

Single experts exercising a co-ordinating role

Another problematic issue yet to be tested in the courts is whether immunity attaches to reports prepared by experts in accordance with paragraph 6 of the Part 35 Practice Direction. This provides that, where a court has ruled that evidence on a particular issue is to be given by a single expert and a number of disciplines are relevant to that issue, an expert in the dominant discipline should be appointed. This expert would then take responsibility for preparing the general part of the report and annexing to it, or incorporating, the contents of any reports from experts in the other disciplines.

When several experts contribute to one report co-ordinated by a lead expert, who is immune?

It is clear that in these circumstances the lead expert would be entitled to immunity in respect of his own report, but can it also protect him from being sued for negligence in the collation and presentation of the reports supplied by the other experts? Furthermore, would the contributing experts be immune from suit for errors or untrue statements in the reports they submitted to the lead expert, given that the court itself had ruled out all possibility of their giving

Lead expert definitely immune in respect of own report

What about immunity of contributing experts?

evidence themselves? Sooner or later, the Court of Appeal is going to have to resolve these issues too.

Human Rights Act 1998

Incorporation of European Convention on Human Rights has caused difficulties

The difficulty in defining the nature and extent of an expert's immunity has been made even greater by the incorporation into UK law of the European Convention on Human Rights. Article 6 of the Convention specifies that:

> '... in the determination of his civil rights... everyone is entitled to... a hearing by a tribunal'.

Previously, any challenge to an immunity on the ground that it denied that right had to be taken to the European Court in Strasbourg. Now, however, such challenges can be mounted in our domestic courts. In ruling on them the courts have to take into account decisions of the European Court of Human Rights (ECHR).

Although the ECHR has never been called upon to consider expert immunity as such, it has dealt with issues arising from other immunities, most notably that enjoyed by the police.

The leading case here is *Osman -v- United Kingdom*[4], which the Court decided in 1998. The applicants had complained that the State had failed to protect the lives of a father and son, one of whom had been murdered and the other injured by the son's teacher. As the police were aware of the danger posed by the teacher, the victims's family had sued them for negligence. When eventually the action reached the Court of Appeal, however, it was struck out on the ground that, for reasons of public

---

[4] *Osman -v- United Kingdom* [1998] *29 EHRR* 245.

policy, the police owe members of the public no duty of care in the investigation and suppression of crime.

In its ruling, the ECHR accepted that the immunity conferred on the police pursued a legitimate aim. It was in the interest of the community at large that police work should not be jeopardised by constant legal challenges to policing policy and operational decisions. That aim had to be proportionate to the means employed to achieve it, however. In this case other considerations needed to be taken into account. These included the gravity of the negligence alleged and the seriousness of the harm suffered. Only by allowing the Osman family's case a hearing could the relative importance of these competing interests be assessed.

The ECHR's ruling in the *Osman* case has far wider ramifications than the law relating to the police, for it undermines blanket immunities of all kinds. The House of Lords has already relied on it to reject those claims to immunity advanced, in separate cases, by a local council and a local education authority. If immunities such as theirs can now be challenged, why not those claimed by, or on behalf of, participants in judicial proceedings such as the Crown Prosecution Service, advocates and expert witnesses?

Real threat posed to expert immunity by ECHR ruling

End of advocate immunity

Although the concept of blanket immunity was already under threat from a number of quarters, it received a knock-out blow in July 2000. The House of Lords ruled that it is no longer in the public interest that advocates should have immunity from suit for negligence in their conduct of cases in court. A team of no fewer than seven law lords heard the combined action, which had been brought by the Solicitors' Indemnity Fund in an effort to overturn a trio of

Advocate immunity for conduct of case withdrawn

decisions the Court of Appeal had handed down in December 1998.[5]

- In *Arthur J S Hall & Co -v- Simons* and *Barratt -v- Woolf Seddon*, the Court of Appeal had allowed the appeals of two clients against decisions of lower courts in striking out claims against their former solicitors.

- In *Harris -v- Scholfield Roberts & Hill*, the Court had dismissed the appeal of a firm of solicitors which had had a claim against it allowed in the High Court.

In all three actions, the clients had alleged negligence in the in-court conduct of still earlier cases of theirs.

Delivering the lead judgment of the House, Lord Hoffmann noted that there had been great changes over the past 30 years in the law of negligence, the administration of justice and public perceptions, and that it was time to look at the issues again. He then reviewed the arguments supportive of the blanket immunity enjoyed by solicitors and barristers in respect of their conduct of cases and had little difficulty in disposing of most of them. The only one he regarded as having real substance was that which held that it was contrary to the public interest to retry a case already decided in another court. However, actions for negligence against lawyers were not the only cases that gave rise to that possibility. Nor was it invariably true that re-litigation of an issue was unfair or brought the administration of justice into disrepute. Furthermore, where re-litigation was an abuse of process, the courts had the power to strike it out.

---

[5] *Arthur J S Hall & Co -v- Simons* [2000] 3 *AER* 673.

Advocate immunity -v- expert immunity

In the course of his judgment, Lord Hoffmann took care to stress that the advocates, like judges and witnesses, enjoy absolute immunity in respect of everything they say in court. He went on to observe, however, that advocates differ from other participants in the judicial process in that they alone owe a duty of care to their clients. It was for that reason that clients should be able to sue them for negligence in the conduct of their cases.

Advocates owe a duty of care to their clients, so clients should be able to sue

In holding that there was no analogy in this respect between the position of advocates and that of judges or witnesses, did Lord Hoffmann overlook the special situation of expert witnesses? As Lord Hobhouse noted in his partly dissenting judgment, their position is very similar to that of advocates. They, too, are selected and paid by the parties instructing them and owe their instructing parties a duty of care in the performance of their duties. If this includes advising the client, and the advice is negligently given, then the expert is just as liable to being sued as would be the lawyer. It is only when the expert becomes engaged in providing expert evidence for use in court that the relationship to the court becomes paramount and the expert enjoys the civil immunity that goes with that function.

Expert advisors not immune, expert witnesses immune

The decision in *Hall -v- Simons* opens a line of argument that threatens the continuance of expert immunity in its present form. It has made the advocate, alone among those participating in the judicial process, liable for what he does or does not say in court. That, as Lord Hobhouse pointed out in his judgment, is tantamount to correcting one anomaly by creating another. Given the similar relationship of advocates and expert witnesses *vis-à-vis* the parties instructing them, it can only be a matter of time before clients alleging negligence on the part of experts attempt to exploit this new anomaly.

Expert properly analogous with the judge

The question of whether an expert has prepared his report with reasonable skill and care is probably one a party is entitled to ask, having regard to the expert's duty to the court. If the expert has failed in this duty, should not he be called to account?

Expert owes duty to the court, so court would have cause for action

The difficulty is, of course, that if the duty is one owed to the court, it should be the court that has the cause of action in negligence, rather than the injured party. Stephen Castell puts it thus:

Expert analogous to judge

'Conceptually, the expert may be said to sit in court beside the judge, not beside his client. It follows that if anyone is to question the expert's standard of work, it should surely be the court alone: the court is, as it were, the only party entitled to say if it considers that the expert's discharge of his or her primary duties to the party has been negligent.' (*Law Letters, The Times,* 25 March 2003)

Expert must not act as advocate

This persuasive point of view is based on the fact that the one thing an expert must not do is to (attempt to) act as an advocate. Unlike an advocate the expert does not, and must not, argue his party's case. Unlike the lawyers in the case, the expert:

- **does not have conduct** of the case
- **gives opinion only**, not advice
- has a **responsibility to (find) the truth**, and
- acts as a **extension to the judge's 'knowledge base'**.

Expert must be unbiased and objective

The expert must provide an unbiased and (wherever possible) objective opinion, based on diligent, rational investigation and analysis. On the basis of his special expertise, he must offer an independent view to the judge to assist the court in determining the issues in the case.

Given the frequency with which it arises, the view that the position of experts is analogous to that of advocates is clearly an attractive line of argument for many lawyers. However, the reality is that expert witnesses are far closer to the judge than the advocates. Accordingly, the removal of immunity from claims of negligence against barristers should have little significance for experts. But, as we will see, that does not mean an expert witness cannot be vexed by other means.

Disciplinary proceedings

There is no rule providing for specific sanctions where an expert witness is in breach of his Part 35 duty. Nor is there any system of accreditation of expert witnesses. There is, therefore, no specific accrediting body to whose attention a breach of expert witness duty can be drawn.

How can an expert witness be reported for breach of duty?

Most (but not all) expert witnesses, however, belong to some form of professional body or institute. Judge Jacob has said that he can see no reason why a judge, who has formed the opinion that an expert has seriously broken his Part 35 duty, should not, in an appropriate case, refer the matter to the expert's professional body, if he has one. Whether there is a breach of the expert's professional rules, and, if so, what sanction is appropriate, would then be a matter for the body concerned.

Report expert to professional body for disciplining

He followed just this course in delivering his judgment in *Gareth Pearce -v- Ove Arup Partnership*

Ltd and Others.[6] In that case he referred the conduct of an expert architect to the Royal Institute of British Architects. The Conduct Committee of the Architects Registration Board subsequently ruled that the architect concerned had not acted improperly. In ordering the referral, however, the trial judge was, in one sense, bypassing the expert's immunity and leaving the way open for another tribunal to make a finding of fault and to impose sanctions.

This is a system other judges might follow in future. But in the view of Mr Justice Collins, it is not one that should be open to anyone else.

The GMC and Professor Sir Roy Meadow

Court can remove the immunity it gives

In 1999, Professor Sir Roy Meadow, a world-renowned authority on paediatrics, gave evidence for the prosecution in the case of Sally Clark, a solicitor accused of murdering her two young children. Four years later, Sally Clark's conviction was quashed by the Court of Appeal[7], at the second time of asking. This decision was based on the fact that a pathologist in the case had failed to recognise the importance of a toxicology report showing signs of infection in the spinal fluid of one of the children.

First Court of Appeal cleared Meadow of any serious fault

The first, unsuccessful, appeal had put forward as one of its grounds that Meadow had misused statistical evidence. He had told the court of the findings of a Government-sponsored study into sudden infant deaths which reported the chance of two 'cot deaths' in one family to be 73,000,000:1. There is now no doubt that the statistic is wrong. But the Court of Appeal took the view that, in the context

---

[6] *Gareth Pearce -v- Ove Arup Partnership Ltd & Anors* [2001] *EWHC* 2 November.

[7] *R -v- Clark* [2003] *EWCA Crim* 1020.

of the trial and the evidential surroundings in which Meadow gave his evidence, the statistic was not capable of having misled the jury.

At the GMC

The Clark family could not accept this. Having secured her release in 2003, they turned their attention back to Meadow. They recognised that immunity protected Meadow from any civil action they might want to take. So they turned instead to the General Medical Council (GMC). Sally Clark's father complained to the GMC and the GMC decided to launch a Fitness to Practice hearing against Meadow.

Clark family complains about Meadow to the GMC

In July 2005, the GMC, having made a finding of fact that Meadow did not intend to mislead, threw the book at Meadow and ruled that he should be struck off the Medical Register. Meadow appealed. Expert immunity appeared in tatters. If professional regulatory bodies could remove a person's right to earn a living in that profession based on his actions as an expert witness, what value was the court-given immunity against civil suit?

GMC decides to remove Meadow from the medical register

At the High Court

In February 2006, Mr Justice Collins, sitting in the Administrative Court[8], ruled against the GMC. Collins J said that not only was the Fitness to Practice Panel (FPP) of the GMC wrong to find Meadow guilty of serious professional misconduct, but that the actions of the FPP verged on the 'irrational' in imposing the ultimate sanction of erasure from the Medical Register.

High Court finds GMC decision 'irrational'

In terms of their general importance, Mr Justice Collins's findings in relation to the GMC pale in

---

[8] *Meadow -v- General Medical Council* [2006] *EWHC Admin* 146.

comparison with his decision to use the Meadow appeal as an opportunity to address, of his own volition, the clear and present danger of professional regulatory bodies outflanking witness immunity.

Collins J took pains to set out the long history of the witness immunity rule, which goes back at least as far as *R -v- Skinner* (1772). It is clear that he wished to leave no doubt as to why the rule exists and its fundamental importance in the proper administration of justice. He went on to point out that its reach encompasses all disciplinary proceedings.

Witness immunity exists to protect the public, not the witness

There is an important principle underpinning the witness immunity rule but which is often overlooked. Witness immunity exists to protect the *public*, not the *witness*. One should not necessarily expect the GMC to understand this, but it is fundamental to the proper determination of whether any shortcoming in a witness is serious enough to warrant action against that witness. This is why it is proper for the court to make that judgment.

Allowing disciplinary bypass of immunity unwise

Immunity for expert witnesses is not a special favour to them. It is just part of the immunity extended to all witnesses. Any defendant who bemoans this protection for an expert witness with whose opinion they disagree ought to reflect on the fact that it also protects those experts whose opinions they favour. Allowing the 'disciplinary bypass' of immunity would inevitably lead to defendants who had access to almost no expert input.

Court should determine if expert has failed in his duties

But, despite what the GMC said in its press release on 17 February 2006, the extended scope of witness immunity does not 'place doctors, and other professionals, beyond the reach of their regulator, when writing reports for the courts or giving evidence.' Expert witnesses owe an overriding duty to the court. It is, therefore, right and proper that it should be for the court to determine whether any particular expert witness has fallen short in performing his expert witness duties.

At the Court of Appeal

However, the GMC was not to be cowed by a mere High Court judge. It went off to the Court of Appeal, and was soon joined by the big guns in the form of the Attorney General, who asked the Court for permission to intervene.

Attorney General intervenes on the basis of public policy

The GMC appeal did not ask for any further action against Meadow, and he will not now be struck off the Medical Register. But to the GMC, the idea that there should be any control on its ability to regulate doctors was anathema. It is that aspect of the Collins J judgment which the GMC, and the Attorney General, sought to overturn.

The hearing took place in July 2006 and the Court of Appeal delivered its judgment at the end of October. On the issue of immunity, the Master of the Rolls (Sir Anthony Clarke) delivered the lead judgment and, supported by Auld LJ and Thorpe LJ (heads of the criminal and family divisions respectively), completely overturned the proposals put forward by Collins.

Court of Appeal overturns Collins

This is a matter of regret to many experts. Collins J's proposals meshed perfectly with the central tenets of the Better Regulation Commission's Principles of Good Regulation, of being proportionate, accountable, consistent, transparent and targeted. His proposals seemed so sensible because they stated that the authority granting the immunity, i.e. the court, was the only authority competent to remove it.

High Court proposal sat well with Better Regulation Commission guidance

On a case-by-case basis, the court could determine whether an expert witness's performance, in the

Case-by-case analysis of an expert's performance

context of the litigation, had slipped so badly as to warrant referral to the appropriate professional body. It would no longer be possible for dissatisfied parties in litigation (or their fathers), often at no cost to themselves, to do a side-run around witness immunity and vex experts with professional disciplinary proceedings.

Professional regulators not left impotent

Nothing in Collins J's decision left professional regulators impotent to deal with seriously flawed experts. Collins simply stated that the court, i.e. the authority granting the immunity, should be the only gatekeeper competent to remove that protection.

At the House of Lords?

Neither Professor Meadow nor the GMC is likely to appeal the decision. However, there remains the question of whether the Medical Defence Union (MDU) would wish to pursue the immunity issue.

The protection from professional disciplinary proceedings set out by Collins J would have valuable consequences for any medical defence body. But the Attorney General's intervention on public policy grounds, and his clearly stated view that any such protection should be a legislative matter and not something for the common law, will cause the MDU to think long and hard before seeking leave to take the immunity point higher.

Effect on the supply of expert witnesses

It is ironic to note that the Court of Appeal has strongly reinforced the view that complaints against medical expert witnesses should be handled by the GMC, the very body which two courts have now found to have wrongly dealt with Professor Meadow!

Ruling risks further reducing pool of experts

The real losers in all this will be those who turn to the courts to help them settle disputes or who are charged with a crime. It will become increasingly difficult to locate competent experts willing to put at risk a primary career for what is essentially an extra-curricular activity.

Costs sanctions

The distinction made in relation to the expert's specific duty to the court (as opposed to a duty owed to any party to the action) has also opened a challenge to expert immunity by another route – that of costs sanctions. But again, it is a route under the control of the courts.

Costs sanctions against experts also an option

In October 2004 the Chancery Division heard an application in relation to preliminary matters in the case of *Phillips & Others -v- Symes & Others*.[9] The questions the court was asked to determine included whether an expert (whose report had been largely discredited and criticised at a previous hearing) could be added as a respondent in the case pursuant to CPR 48.2 for the purpose of costs only.

Can discredited expert be added as respondent in case for costs?

The facts of the case were complex. Put simply, it was argued that the case would never have come to trial but for the expert's allegedly inadequate report. Although the applicants had ultimately been successful, they were faced with a huge legal bill which they had little chance of recovering. Consequently, they sought an order for costs against the expert who, they said, had breached his overriding duty to the court.

A competent report would have settled the case before trial

In considering the application Mr Justice Peter Smith was at pains to point out that he was not making any finding against the expert that was tantamount to a finding of breach of duty or negligence. The purpose of the preliminary hearing was merely to decide

---

[9] *Phillips & Others -v- Symes & Others (Costs No. 2)* [2004] EWHC 2330 (Ch).

whether, as a matter of law, it was possible to add the expert to the proceedings and for an application for costs against the expert to be subsequently considered.

Consequences of breaching duty

An expert owes his duty to the court. An expert is required to assist the court, to behave objectively and not to be partisan. An expert is not to act as a hired gun for the party. But what are the consequences of breaching that duty? The court summarised these as follows:

Expert charged with perjury or contempt of court

- First, an expert can be said to be in **contempt of court, or even guilty of perjury**, depending on the extent of their dereliction.

Expert's costs disallowed

- Second, it might be possible in an appropriate case to order that the **expert's costs be disallowed**. In this context the costs can be either those between the expert's 'client' and another party to the litigation, or those between the client and the expert.

Expert referred to professional body

- Third, the behaviour of the expert can be a matter for **referral to the expert's professional body** (if there is one). This was the course taken by Judge Jacobs in *Gareth Pierce -v- Ove Arup*.

The applicants argued that none of these provided a sanction that would compensate the true 'victim' of the expert's breach of duty, namely the other parties. They further argued that the development of the law in relation to the ability to order payment of costs by non-parties meant that it was now possible for the courts to order experts to pay compensation to parties who had suffered loss 'by reason of their gross dereliction of duty'.

The court referred back to the 'witness analogy' cited in Lord Hoffmann's judgment in *Arthur J S Hall*. The conclusion was that it is not sufficient to explain any immunity by saying that the people involved should be free from avoidable strain and tensions. The rule in relation to immunity of witnesses depends upon the proposition that, without it, witnesses would be more reluctant to assist the court.

It was submitted that the position of experts was analogous to that of advocates, who have long been subject to sanctions as regards wasted costs orders. Representing the applicants, Mr A Steinfeld, QC, described experts as being 'quasi Officers of the Court'. He said that, in the modern world, there should be an effective sanction capable of being imposed on them.

The rule in relation to immunity of witnesses depends upon the proposition that, without it, witnesses would be more reluctant to assist the court. In *Stanton -v- Callaghan* the Court of Appeal held that an expert witness could not be sued for agreeing to a joint expert statement in terms the client considered to be detrimental to his interests. This was postulated on the general principle of witness immunity: that the administration of justice would be adversely affected if witnesses felt unable to give their evidence freely and without fear. Mr Justice Peter Smith agreed that there was a need for witnesses to give their evidence freely, but he considered that although this right was paramount, it was not absolute. Indeed, blanket immunity had been discouraged by the ECHR since the *Osman* decision, and each case must now be considered on its own merits.

Without immunity, witnesses would be more reluctant to assist court

If witnesses tell lies, they can be prosecuted for perjury; if they sign a false declaration of truth to a witness statement, they can also be held in contempt of court. An expert who signs a false declaration is equally open to contempt proceedings.

Lies and false declarations already have their own remedy

Litigation seeking damages due to evidence given not allowed

What is currently prohibited is litigation seeking damages or other remedy arising out of the evidence itself.

The expert witness chooses to be a witness. In this way experts differ from lay witnesses. Unlike lay witnesses, experts are paid, professional and uncompellable. Why, then, should immunity be regarded as a necessary corollary of independence?

If the expert is not to be held liable for professional negligence if he is incompetent or if he fails in his duty to the court, should there be a compromise remedy in the shape of a wasted costs order? This would, at least, give the criticised expert an opportunity to defend himself before the judge at a proper hearing.

Can experts be the subject of wasted costs orders?

The judge considered the question to be posed was 'Do expert witnesses need immunity from a costs application against them as a furtherance of the administration of justice?' Although there was nothing in the *Arthur J S Hall* and *Stanton* cases to suggest that a witness could be made subject to an order for costs, there was equally nothing to say that they could not.

Judge Smith said that, in his judgment, the question should be looked at in the light of modern developments of the law in relation to litigation. The courts had already decided that loss of immunity would not prevent advocates from fearlessly representing their clients. Wasted costs applications against advocates had been decoupled from immunity and this had effectively destroyed immunity for advocates. In *Stanton*, the Court of Appeal had been equally dismissive of the belief that experts would be deterred from giving proper evidence because of a potential action against them.

In view of the clearly defined duties enshrined in CPR Part 35 and its Practice Direction, it would be wrong, said the judge, for the court to remove from itself the power to make a costs order against an expert who, by his evidence, causes significant expense to be incurred and does so 'in flagrant, reckless disregard of his duties to the Court'. He did not believe that the other available sanctions were effective or anything other than 'blunt instruments'. The proper sanction was, in his view, the ability to compensate a person who has suffered loss as a result.

The answer is 'Yes!'

The judge did not accept that experts would be inhibited from performing their duties by reason of a potential exposure to costs. That, he said, was a *crie de coer* often made by professionals. Any suggestion that the floodgates would be opened was one that was unlikely to carry any real weight because this failed to take account of the very high level of proof that would be required to establish the breach of duty. The floodgates argument had failed with regards lawyers, and the judge did not believe that the position of experts would be any different.

Professional indemnity insurance

It is, of course, one thing to be held liable for negligence and quite another to be proved negligent. Furthermore, in criminal proceedings the rule against abusive collateral attack should mean that convicted defendants would be unable to sue their experts unless, and until, their convictions had been quashed. The decision in *Hall -v- Simons* and events since then have, however, increased the likelihood of more claims being made against experts in the wake of failed civil proceedings. The need for experts to insure themselves against that possibility, even if

PI insurance an essential safeguard

only for the defence costs, is now greater than ever –
if only to ensure a good night's sleep!

Appendices

Appendix 1: CPR Part 35

The following is taken from the 43rd update of the Rules dated December 2006.

35.1 Duty to restrict expert evidence

Expert evidence shall be restricted to that which is reasonably required to resolve the proceedings.

35.2 Interpretation

A reference to an 'expert' in this Part is a reference to an expert who has been instructed to give or prepare evidence for the purpose of court proceedings.

35.3 Experts – overriding duty to the court

(1) It is the duty of an expert to help the court on the matters within his expertise.

(2) This duty overrides any obligation to the person from whom he has received instructions or by whom he is paid.

35.4 Court's power to restrict expert evidence

(1) No party may call an expert or put in evidence an expert's report without the court's permission.

(2) When a party applies for permission under this rule he must identify –

(a) the field in which he wishes to rely on expert evidence; and

(b) where practicable the expert in that field on whose evidence he wishes to rely.

(3) If permission is granted under this rule it shall be in relation only to the expert named or the field identified under paragraph (2).

(4) The court may limit the amount of the expert's fees and expenses that the party who wishes to rely on the expert may recover from any other party.

35.5 General requirement for expert evidence to be given in a written report

(1)   Expert evidence is to be given in a written report unless the court directs otherwise.

(2)   If a claim is on the fast track, the court will not direct an expert to attend a hearing unless it is necessary to do so in the interests of justice.

35.6 Written questions to experts

(1)   A party may put to –
   (a)   an expert instructed by another party; or
   (b)   a single joint expert appointed under rule 35.7
   written questions about his report.

(2)   Written questions under paragraph (1) –
   (a)   may be put once only;
   (b)   must be put within 28 days of service of the expert's report; and,
   (c)   must be for the purpose only of clarification of the report,
   unless in any case –
      (i)   the court gives permission; or
      (ii)   the other party agrees.

(3)   An expert's answers to questions put in accordance with paragraph (1) shall be treated as part of the expert's report.

(4)   Where –
   (a)   a party has put a written question to an expert instructed by another party in accordance with this rule; and
   (b)   the expert does not answer that question,
   the court may make one or both of the following orders in relation to the party who instructed the expert –
      (i)   that the party may not rely on the evidence of that expert; or
      (ii)   that the party may not recover the fees and expenses of that expert from any other party.

35.7 Court's power to direct that evidence is to be given by a single joint expert

(1)   Where two or more parties wish to submit expert evidence on a particular issue, the court may direct that the evidence on that issue is to given by one expert only.

(2)   The parties wishing to submit the expert evidence are called 'the instructing parties'.

(3)   Where the instructing parties cannot agree who should be the expert, the court may –
   (a)   select the expert from a list prepared or identified by the instructing parties; or
   (b)   direct that the expert be selected in such other manner as the court may direct.

35.8 Instructions to a single joint expert

(1) Where the court gives a direction under rule 35.7 for a single joint expert to be used, each instructing party may give instructions to the expert.

(2) When an instructing party gives instructions to the expert he must, at the same time, send a copy of the instructions to the other instructing parties.

(3) The court may give directions about –

    (a) the payment of the expert's fees and expenses; and

    (b) any inspection, examination or experiments which the expert wishes to carry out.

(4) The court may, before an expert is instructed –

    (a) limit the amount that can be paid by way of fees and expenses to the expert; and

    (b) direct that the instructing parties pay that amount into court.

(5) Unless the court otherwise directs, the instructing parties are jointly and severally liable for the payment of the expert's fees and expenses.

35.9 Power of court to direct a party to provide information

(1) Where a party has access to information which is not reasonably available to the other party, the court may direct the party who has access to the information to –

    (a) prepare and file a document recording the information; and

    (b) serve a copy of that document on the other party.

35.10 Contents of report

(1) An expert's report must comply with the requirements set out in the relevant practice direction.

(2) At the end of an expert's report there must be a statement that –

    (a) the expert understands his duty to the court; and

    (b) he has complied with that duty.

(3) The expert's report must state the substance of all material instructions, whether written or oral, on the basis of which the report was written.

(4) The instructions referred to in paragraph (3) shall not be privileged against disclosure but the court will not, in relation to those instructions –

    (a) order disclosure of any specific document; or

    (b) permit any questioning in court, other than by the party who instructed the expert,

unless it is satisfied that there are reasonable grounds to consider the statement of instructions given under paragraph (3) to be inaccurate or incomplete.

35.11 Use by one party of expert's report disclosed by another

(1)   Where a party has disclosed an expert's report, any party may use that expert's report as evidence at the trial.

35.12 Discussions between experts

(1)   The court may, at any stage, direct a discussion between experts for the purpose of requiring the experts to –
   (a)   identify and discuss the expert issues in the proceedings; and
   (b)   where possible, reach an agreed opinion on those issues.

(2)   The court may specify the issues which the experts must discuss.

(3)   The court may direct that following a discussion between the experts they must prepare a statement for the court showing –
   (a)   those issues on which they agree; and
   (b)   those issues on which they disagree and a summary of their reasons for disagreeing.

(4)   The content of the discussion between the experts shall not be referred to at the trial unless the parties agree.

(5)   Where experts reach agreement on an issue during their discussions, the agreement shall not bind the parties unless the parties expressly agree to be bound by the agreement.

35.13 Consequence of failure to disclose expert's report

(1)   A party who fails to disclose an expert's report may not use the report at the trial or call the expert to give evidence orally unless the court gives permission.

35.14 Expert's right to ask court for directions

(1)   An expert may file a written request for directions to assist him in carrying out his function as an expert.

(2)   An expert must, unless the court orders otherwise, provide a copy of any proposed request for directions under paragraph (1) –
   (a)   to the party instructing him, at least 7 days before he files the request; and
   (b)   to all other parties, at least 4 days before he files it.

(3)   The court, when it gives directions, may also direct that a party be served with a copy of the directions.

35.15 Assessors

(1)   This rule applies where the court appoints one or more persons (an 'assessor') under section 70 of the Supreme Court Act 1981 or section 63 of the County Courts Act 1984.

(2)   The assessor shall assist the court in dealing with a matter in which the assessor has skill and experience.

(3) An assessor shall take such part in the proceedings as the court may direct and in particular the court may –
   (a) direct the assessor to prepare a report for the court on any matter at issue in the proceedings; and
   (b) direct the assessor to attend the whole or any part of the trial to advise the court on any such matter.

(4) If the assessor prepares a report for the court before the trial has begun –
   (a) the court will send a copy to each of the parties; and
   (b) the parties may use it at trial.

(5) The remuneration to be paid to the assessor for his services shall be determined by the court and shall form part of the costs of the proceedings.

(6) The court may order any party to deposit in the court office a specified sum in respect of the assessor's fees and, where it does so, the assessor will not be asked to act until the sum has been deposited.

(7) Paragraphs (5) and (6) do not apply where the remuneration of the assessor is to be paid out of money provided by Parliament.

Appendix 2: CPR Part 35 Practice Direction

The following is taken from the 43rd update of the Rules dated December 2006.

Part 35 is intended to limit the use of oral expert evidence to that which is reasonably required. In addition, where possible, matters requiring expert evidence should be dealt with by a single expert. Permission of the court is always required either to call an expert or to put an expert's report in evidence. There is annexed to this Practice Direction [see page 194] a protocol for the instruction of experts to give evidence in civil claims. Experts and those instructing them are expected to have regard to the guidance contained in the protocol.

Expert evidence – general requirements

1.1 It is the duty of an expert to help the court on matters within his own expertise: rule 35.3(1). This duty is paramount and overrides any obligation to the person from whom the expert has received instructions or by whom he is paid: rule 35.3(2).

1.2 Expert evidence should be the independent product of the expert uninfluenced by the pressures of litigation.

1.3 An expert should assist the court by providing objective, unbiased opinion on matters within his expertise, and should not assume the role of an advocate.

1.4 An expert should consider all material facts, including those which might detract from his opinion.

1.5 An expert should make it clear:
   (a) when a question or issue falls outside his expertise; and
   (b) when he is not able to reach a definite opinion, for example because he has insufficient information.

1.6 If, after producing a report, an expert changes his view on any material matter, such change of view should be communicated to all the parties without delay, and when appropriate to the court.

Form and content of expert's reports

2.1 An expert's report should be addressed to the court and not to the party from whom the expert has received his instructions.

2.2 An expert's report must:
   (1) give details of the expert's qualifications;
   (2) give details of any literature or other material which the expert has relied on in making the report;
   (3) contain a statement setting out the substance of all facts and instructions given to the expert which are

material to the opinions expressed in the report or upon which those opinions are based;

(4)   make clear which of the facts stated in the report are within the expert's own knowledge;

(5)   say who carried out any examination, measurement, test or experiment which the expert has used for the report, give the qualifications of that person, and say whether or not the test or experiment has been carried out under the expert's supervision;

(6)   where there is a range of opinion on the matters dealt with in the report –

(a) summarise the range of opinion, and

(b) give reasons for his own opinion;

(7)   contain a summary of the conclusions reached;

(8)   if the expert is not able to give his opinion without qualification, state the qualification; and

(9)   contain a statement that the expert understands his duty to the court, and has complied and will continue to comply with that duty.

2.3   An expert's report must be verified by a statement of truth, as well as containing the statements required in paragraph 2.2 (8) and (9) above.

2.4   The form of the statement of truth is as follows: 'I confirm that insofar as the facts stated in my report are within my own knowledge I have made clear which they are and I believe them to be true, and that the opinions I have expressed represent my true and complete professional opinion.'

2.5   Attention is drawn to rule 32.14, which sets out the consequences of verifying a document containing a false statement without an honest belief in its truth.

(For information about statements of truth see Part 22 and the practice direction which supplements it.)

Information

3   Under Rule 35.9 the court may direct a party with access to information which is not reasonably available to another party to serve on that other party a document which records the information. The document served must include sufficient details of all the facts, tests, experiments and assumptions which underlie any part of the information to enable the party on whom it is served to make, or to obtain, a proper interpretation of the information and an assessment of its significance.

Instructions

4   The instructions referred to in paragraph 2.2(3) will not be protected by privilege [see rule 35.10(4)]. But cross-examination of the expert on the contents of his

instructions will not be allowed unless the court permits it (or unless the party who gave the instructions consents to it). Before it gives permission the court must be satisfied that there are reasonable grounds to consider that the statement in the report of the substance of the instructions is inaccurate or incomplete. If the court is so satisfied, it will allow the cross-examination where it appears to be in the interests of justice to do so.

Questions to experts

5.1 Questions asked for the purpose of clarifying the expert's report (see rule 35.6) should be put, in writing, to the expert not later than 28 days after receipt of the expert's report (see paragraphs 1.2 to 1.5 above as to verification).

5.2 Where a party sends a written question or questions direct to an expert, a copy of the questions should, at the same time, be sent to the other party or parties.

5.3 The party or parties instructing the expert must pay any fees charged by that expert for answering questions put under rule 35.6. This does not affect any decision of the court as to the party who is ultimately to bear the expert's costs.

Single expert

6 Where the court has directed that the evidence on a particular issue is to be given by one expert only (rule 35.7) but there are a number of disciplines relevant to that issue, a leading expert in the dominant discipline should be identified as the single expert. He should prepare the general part of the report and be responsible for annexing or incorporating the contents of any reports from experts in other disciplines.

Orders

6a Where an order requires an act to be done by an expert, or otherwise affects an expert, the party instructing that expert must serve a copy of the order on the expert instructed by him. In the case of a jointly instructed expert, the claimant must serve the order.

Assessors

7.1 An assessor may be appointed to assist the court under rule 35.15. Not less than 21 days before making any such appointment, the court will notify each party in writing of the name of the proposed assessor, of the matter in respect of which the assistance of the assessor will be sought and of the qualifications of the assessor to give that assistance.

7.2 Where any person has been proposed for appointment as an assessor, objection to him, either personally or in respect of his qualification, may be taken by any party.

7.3 Any such objection must be made in writing and filed with the court within 7 days of receipt of the notification referred to in paragraph 7.1 and will be taken into account by the court in deciding whether or not to make the appointment (section 63(5) of the County Courts Act 1984).

7.4 Copies of any report prepared by the assessor will be sent to each of the parties but the assessor will not give oral evidence or be open to cross-examination or questioning.

Appendix 3: Annotated CJC Experts Protocol

The *UK Register of Expert Witnesses* is delighted that the Civil Justice Council (CJC) has taken the initiative – cutting through the confusion created by the regrettable inability of the Academy of Experts and Expert Witness Institute to work together – to establish a single, authoritative Experts Protocol. The expert witness community should welcome this development.

Having worked through the Protocol in some detail, we have identified a number of areas where further guidance may assist expert witnesses. This assertion is based upon the evidence we have gathered from our helpline – what actually troubles expert witnesses enough that they contact us. We are told, by its authors, that the Protocol cannot be modified (which seems a shame since any protocol ought to be capable of reflecting the developing needs of its constituency). We have been forced, therefore, to publish below an annotated version of the Protocol that includes these additional points of guidance. It clearly differentiates the official text from our annotations (shown in call out boxes).

1. Introduction

1.1   Expert witnesses perform a vital role in civil litigation. It is essential that both those who instruct experts and experts themselves are given clear guidance as to what they are expected to do in civil proceedings. The purpose of this Protocol is to provide such guidance. It has been drafted by the Civil Justice Council and reflects the rules and practice directions current [in June 2005], replacing the Code of Guidance on Expert Evidence. The authors of the Protocol wish to acknowledge the valuable assistance they obtained by drawing on earlier documents produced by the Academy of Experts and the Expert Witness Institute, as well as suggestions made by the Clinical Dispute Forum. The Protocol has been approved by the Master of the Rolls.

2. Aims of Protocol

2.1   This Protocol offers guidance to experts and to those instructing them in the interpretation of and compliance with Part 35 of the Civil Procedure Rules (CPR 35) and its associated Practice Direction (PD 35) and to further the objectives of the Civil Procedure Rules in general. It is intended to assist in the interpretation of those provisions in the interests of good practice but it does not replace them. It sets out standards for the use of experts and the conduct of experts and those who instruct them. The existence of this

Protocol does not remove the need for experts and those who instruct them to be familiar with CPR35 and PD35.

2.2 Experts and those who instruct them should also bear in mind para 1.4 of the Practice Direction on Protocols which contains the following objectives, namely to:

(a) encourage the exchange of early and full information about the expert issues involved in a prospective legal claim;

(b) enable the parties to avoid or reduce the scope of litigation by agreeing the whole or part of an expert issue before commencement of proceedings; and

(c) support the efficient management of proceedings where litigation cannot be avoided.

3. Application

3.1 This Protocol applies to any steps taken for the purpose of civil proceedings by experts or those who instruct them on or after 5th September 2005.

3.2 It applies to all experts who are, or who may be, governed by CPR Part 35 and to those who instruct them. Experts are governed by Part 35 if they are or have been instructed to give or prepare evidence for the purpose of civil proceedings in a court in England and Wales (CPR 35.2).

3.3 Experts, and those instructing them, should be aware that some cases may be "specialist proceedings" (CPR 49) where there are modifications to the Civil Procedure Rules. Proceedings may also be governed by other Protocols. Further, some courts have published their own Guides which supplement the Civil Procedure Rules for proceedings in those courts. They contain provisions affecting expert evidence. Expert witnesses and those instructing them should be familiar with them when they are relevant.

3.4 Courts may take into account any failure to comply with this Protocol when making orders in relation to costs, interest, time limits, the stay of proceedings and whether to order a party to pay a sum of money into court.

Limitation

3.5 If, as a result of complying with any part of this Protocol, claims would or might be time barred under any provision in the Limitation Act 1980, or any other legislation that imposes a time limit for the bringing of an action, claimants may commence proceedings without complying with this Protocol. In such circumstances, claimants who commence proceedings without complying with all, or any part, of this Protocol must apply, giving notice to all other parties, to the court for directions as to the timetable and form of procedure to be adopted, at the same time as they request the court to issue proceedings. The court may consider whether to order a stay of the whole or part of the proceedings pending compliance with this Protocol and may make orders in relation to costs.

Privilege and Disclosure: Assume no privilege would be claimed

An expert must not be given any information that is legally privileged unless it has been decided that privilege should be waived. An expert should therefore assume that his instructions do not contain any information for which privilege would be claimed.

4. Duties of Experts

4.1   Experts always owe a duty to exercise reasonable skill and care to those instructing them, and to comply with any relevant professional code of ethics. However when they are instructed to give or prepare evidence for the purpose of civil proceedings in England and Wales they have an overriding duty to help the court on matters within their expertise (CPR 35.3). This duty overrides any obligation to the person instructing or paying them. Experts must not serve the exclusive interest of those who retain them.

4.2   Experts should be aware of the overriding objective that courts deal with cases justly. This includes dealing with cases proportionately, expeditiously and fairly (CPR 1.1). Experts are under an obligation to assist the court so as to enable them to deal with cases in accordance with the overriding objective. However the overriding objective does not impose on experts any duty to act as mediators between the parties or require them to trespass on the role of the court in deciding facts.

4.3   Experts should provide opinions which are independent, regardless of the pressures of litigation. In this context, a useful test of 'independence' is that the expert would express the same opinion if given the same instructions by an opposing party. Experts should not take it upon themselves to promote the point of view of the party instructing them or engage in the role of advocates.

4.4   Experts should confine their opinions to matters which are material to the disputes between the parties and provide opinions only in relation to matters which lie within their expertise. Experts should indicate without delay where particular questions or issues fall outside their expertise.

4.5   Experts should take into account all material facts before them at the time that they give their opinion. Their reports should set out those facts and any literature or any other material on which they have relied in forming their opinions.

They should indicate if an opinion is provisional, or qualified, or where they consider that further information is required or if, for any other reason, they are not satisfied that an opinion can be expressed finally and without qualification.

4.6 Experts should inform those instructing them without delay of any change in their opinions on any material matter and the reason for it.

4.7 Experts should be aware that any failure by them to comply with the Civil Procedure Rules or court orders or any excessive delay for which they are responsible may result in the parties who instructed them being penalised in costs and even, in extreme cases, being debarred from placing the experts' evidence before the court. In Phillips v Symes[1] Peter Smith J held that courts may also make orders for costs (under section 51 of the Supreme Court Act 1981) directly against expert witnesses who by their evidence cause significant expense to be incurred, and do so in flagrant and reckless disregard of their duties to the Court.

5. Conduct of Experts instructed only to Advise

5.1 Part 35 only applies where experts are instructed to give opinions which are relied on for the purposes of court proceedings. Advice which the parties do not intend to adduce in litigation is likely to be confidential; the Protocol does not apply in these circumstances.[2] [3]

5.2 The same applies where, after the commencement of proceedings, experts are instructed only to advise (e.g. to comment upon a single joint expert's report) and not to give or prepare evidence for use in the proceedings.

5.3 However this Protocol does apply if experts who were formerly instructed only to advise are later instructed to give or prepare evidence for the purpose of civil proceedings.

6. The Need for Experts

6.1 Those intending to instruct experts to give or prepare evidence for the purpose of civil proceedings should consider whether expert evidence is appropriate, taking account of the principles set out in CPR Parts 1 and 35, and in particular whether:

(a) it is relevant to a matter which is in dispute between the parties;

(b) it is reasonably required to resolve the proceedings (CPR 35.1);

---

[1] *Phillips & Others -v- Symes & Others* [2004] *EWHC* 2330 (Ch).

[2] *Carlson -v- Townsend* [2001] *EWCA Civ* 511.

[3] *Jackson -v- Marley Davenport* [2004] *EWCA Civ* 1225.

    (c)   the expert has expertise relevant to the issue on which an opinion is sought;

    (d)   the expert has the experience, expertise and training appropriate to the value, complexity and importance of the case; and whether

    (e)   these objects can be achieved by the appointment of a single joint expert (see section 17 below).

6.2   Although the court's permission is not generally required to instruct an expert, the court's permission is required before experts can be called to give evidence or their evidence can be put in (CPR 35.4).

7. The Appointment of Experts

7.1   Before experts are formally instructed or the court's permission to appoint named experts is sought, the following should be established:

    (a)   that they have the appropriate expertise and experience;

    (b)   that they are familiar with the general duties of an expert;

    (c)   that they can produce a report, deal with questions and have discussions with other experts within a reasonable time and at a cost proportionate to the matters in issue;

    (d)   a description of the work required;

    (e)   whether they are available to attend the trial, if attendance is required; and

    (f)   there is no potential conflict of interest.

7.2   Terms of appointment should be agreed at the outset and should normally include:

    (a)   the capacity in which the expert is to be appointed (e.g. party appointed expert, single joint expert or expert advisor);

    (b)   the services required of the expert (e.g. provision of expert's report, answering questions in writing, attendance at meetings and attendance at court);

    (c)   time for delivery of the report;

    (d)   the basis of the expert's charges (either daily or hourly rates and an estimate of the time likely to be required, or a total fee for the services);

    (e)   travelling expenses and disbursements;

    (f)   cancellation charges;

    (g)   any fees for attending court;

    (h)   time for making the payment;

    (i)   whether fees are to be paid by a third party; and

    (j)   if a party is publicly funded, whether or not the expert's charges will be subject to assessment by a costs officer.

7.3   As to the appointment of single joint experts, see section 17 below.

7.4   When necessary, arrangements should be made for dealing with questions to experts and discussions between experts, including any directions given by the court, and provision should be made for the cost of this work.

7.5   Experts should be informed regularly about deadlines for all matters concerning them. Those instructing experts should promptly send them copies of all court orders and directions which may affect the preparation of their reports or any other matters concerning their obligations.

Conditional and contingency fees

7.6   Payments contingent upon the nature of the expert evidence given in legal proceedings, or upon the outcome of a case, must not be offered or accepted. To do so would contravene the experts' overriding duty to the court and compromise their duty of independence.

Solicitors should not offer such terms anyway
It should be remembered that the Law Society's Guide to the Professional Conduct of Solicitors specifically states at 21.11 that *'A solicitor must not make or offer to make payments to a witness contingent upon the nature of the evidence given or upon the outcome of a case'.*

7.7   Agreement to delay payment of experts' fees until after the conclusion of cases is permissible as long as the amount of the fee does not depend on the outcome of the case.

8. Instructions

8.1   Those instructing experts should ensure that they give clear instructions, including the following:

(a)   basic information, such as names, addresses, telephone numbers, dates of birth and dates of incidents;

(b)   the nature and extent of the expertise which is called for;

(c)   the purpose of requesting the advice or report, a description of the matter(s) to be investigated, the principal known issues and the identity of all parties;

(d)   the statement(s) of case (if any), those documents which form part of standard disclosure and witness statements which are relevant to the advice or report;

(e)   where proceedings have not been started, whether proceedings are being contemplated and, if so, whether the expert is asked only for advice;

(f)   an outline programme, consistent with good case management and the expert's availability, for the completion and delivery of each stage of the expert's work; and

(g) where proceedings have been started, the dates of any hearings (including any Case Management Conferences and/or Pre-Trial Reviews), the name of the court, the claim number and the track to which the claim has been allocated.

8.2 Experts who do not receive clear instructions should request clarification and may indicate that they are not prepared to act unless and until such clear instructions are received.

8.3 As to the instruction of single joint experts, see section 17 below.

9. Experts' Acceptance of Instructions

9.1 Experts should confirm without delay whether or not they accept instructions. They should also inform those instructing them (whether on initial instruction or at any later stage) without delay if:

(a) instructions are not acceptable because, for example, they require work that falls outside their expertise, impose unrealistic deadlines, or are insufficiently clear;

(b) they consider that instructions are or have become insufficient to complete the work;

(c) they become aware that they may not be able to fulfil any of the terms of appointment;

(d) the instructions and/or work have, for any reason, placed them in conflict with their duties as an expert; or

(e) they are not satisfied that they can comply with any orders that have been made.

Obtain all relevant material

Once he has accepted instructions, the expert should request any material relevant to his consideration of the case that has not already been provided.

If a time limit has been imposed for delivery of the report, an expert's task can be made more difficult if he accepts instructions but then has to wait for a party to furnish him with missing material. For this reason, an expert may prefer to only formally accept the instruction once all the material relevant to his consideration has been delivered.

9.2 Experts must neither express an opinion outside the scope of their field of expertise, nor accept any instructions to do so.

10. Withdrawal

10.1 Where experts' instructions remain incompatible with their
duties, whether through incompleteness, a conflict between
their duty to the court and their instructions, or for any other
substantial and significant reason, they may consider
withdrawing from the case. However, experts should not
withdraw without first discussing the position fully with those
who instruct them and considering carefully whether it would
be more appropriate to make a written request for directions
from the court. If experts do withdraw, they must give formal
written notice to those instructing them.

11. Experts' Right to ask Court for Directions

11.1 Experts may request directions from the court to assist them
in carrying out their functions as experts. Experts should
normally discuss such matters with those who instruct them
before making any such request. Unless the court otherwise
orders, any proposed request for directions should be
copied to the party instructing the expert at least seven days
before filing any request to the court, and to all other parties
at least four days before filing it (CPR 35.14).

11.2 Requests to the court for directions should be made by
letter, containing:

(a)   the title of the claim;

(b)   the claim number of the case;

(c)   the name of the expert;

(d)   full details of why directions are sought; and

(e)   copies of any relevant documentation.

In extremis

In very exceptional circumstances, experts may file with the court
a written request for directions to assist them in carrying out their
function as experts.

It is difficult to see circumstances where this course of action
would be either justified or desirable from the expert's perspective.
The expert works under instruction. If he has any difficulty with his
instructions, he should stop working and seek clarification from
those who instruct him. If they cannot resolve the problem, it is for
the instructing party or parties to seek directions from the court.

**12. Power of the Court to Direct a Party to Provide
Information**

12.1 If experts consider that those instructing them have not
provided information which they require, they may, after
discussion with those instructing them and giving notice,
write to the court to seek directions (CPR 35.14).

12.2 Experts and those who instruct them should also be aware
of CPR 35.9. This provides that where one party has access

to information which is not readily available to the other party, the court may direct the party who has access to the information to prepare, file and copy to the other party a document recording the information. If experts require such information which has not been disclosed, they should discuss the position with those instructing them without delay, so that a request for the information can be made, and, if not forthcoming, an application can be made to the court. Unless a document appears to be essential, experts should assess the cost and time involved in the production of a document and whether its provision would be proportionate in the context of the case.

13. Contents of Experts' Reports

13.1 The content and extent of experts' reports should be governed by the scope of their instructions and general obligations, the contents of CPR 35 and PD35 and their overriding duty to the court.

13.2 In preparing reports, experts should maintain professional objectivity and impartiality at all times.

13.3 PD 35, para 2 provides that experts' reports should be addressed to the court and gives detailed directions about the form and content of such reports. All experts and those who instruct them should ensure that they are familiar with these requirements.

13.4 Model forms of Experts' Reports are available from bodies such as the Academy of Experts or the Expert Witness Institute.

13.5 Experts' reports must contain statements that they understand their duty to the court and have complied and will continue to comply with that duty [PD35 para 2.2(9)]. They must also be verified by a statement of truth. The form of the statement of truth is as follows:
"I confirm that insofar as the facts stated in my report are within my own knowledge I have made clear which they are and I believe them to be true, and that the opinions I have expressed represent my true and complete professional opinion."
This wording is mandatory and must not be modified.

Qualifications

13.6 The details of experts' qualifications to be given in reports should be commensurate with the nature and complexity of the case. It may be sufficient merely to state academic and professional qualifications. However, where highly specialised expertise is called for, experts should include the detail of particular training and/or experience that qualifies them to provide that highly specialised evidence.

Tests

13.7 Where tests of a scientific or technical nature have been carried out, experts should state:

(a)   the methodology used; and

(b)   by whom the tests were undertaken and under whose supervision, summarising their respective qualifications and experience.

Reliance on the work of others

13.8 Where experts rely in their reports on literature or other material and cite the opinions of others without having verified them, they must give details of those opinions relied on. It is likely to assist the court if the qualifications of the originator(s) are also stated.

Facts

13.9 When addressing questions of fact and opinion, experts should keep the two separate and discrete.

13.10 Experts must state those facts (whether assumed or otherwise) upon which their opinions are based. They must distinguish clearly between those facts which experts know to be true and those facts which they assume.

13.11 Where there are material facts in dispute experts should express separate opinions on each hypothesis put forward. They should not express a view in favour of one or other disputed version of the facts unless, as a result of particular expertise and experience, they consider one set of facts as being improbable or less probable, in which case they may express that view, and should give reasons for holding it.

Range of opinion

13.12 If the mandatory summary of the range of opinion is based on published sources, experts should explain those sources and, where appropriate, state the qualifications of the originator(s) of the opinions from which they differ, particularly if such opinions represent a well-established school of thought.

13.13 Where there is no available source for the range of opinion, experts may need to express opinions on what they believe to be the range which other experts would arrive at if asked. In those circumstances, experts should make it clear that the range that they summarise is based on their own judgement and explain the basis of that judgement.

Conclusions

13.14 A summary of conclusions is mandatory. The summary should be at the end of the report after all the reasoning. There may be cases, however, where the benefit to the court is heightened by placing a short summary at the beginning of the report whilst giving the full conclusions at the end. For example, it can assist with the comprehension of the analysis and with the absorption of the detailed facts if the court is told at the outset of the direction in which the report's logic will flow in cases involving highly complex matters which fall outside the general knowledge of the court.

Basis of report: material instructions

13.15 The mandatory statement of the substance of all material instructions should not be incomplete or otherwise tend to mislead. The imperative is transparency. The term "instructions" includes all material which solicitors place in front of experts in order to gain advice. The omission from the statement of 'off-the-record' oral instructions is not permitted. Courts may allow cross-examination about the instructions if there are reasonable grounds to consider that the statement may be inaccurate or incomplete.

14. After Receipt of Experts' Reports

14.1 Following the receipt of experts' reports, those instructing them should advise the experts as soon as reasonably practicable whether, and if so when, the report will be disclosed to other parties; and, if so disclosed, the date of actual disclosure.

14.2 If experts' reports are to be relied upon, and if experts are to give oral evidence, those instructing them should give the experts the opportunity to consider and comment upon other reports within their area of expertise and which deal with relevant issues at the earliest opportunity.

14.3 Those instructing experts should keep experts informed of the progress of cases, including amendments to statements of case relevant to experts' opinion.

14.4 If those instructing experts become aware of material changes in circumstances or that relevant information within their control was not previously provided to experts, they should without delay instruct experts to review, and if necessary update, the contents of their reports.

15. Amendment of Reports

15.1 It may become necessary for experts to amend their reports:
    (a)   as a result of an exchange of questions and answers;
    (b)   following agreements reached at meetings between experts; or
    (c)   where further evidence or documentation is disclosed.

15.2 Experts should not be asked to, and should not, amend, expand or alter any parts of reports in a manner which distorts their true opinion, but may be invited to amend or expand reports to ensure accuracy, internal consistency, completeness and relevance to the issues and clarity.

Although experts should generally follow the recommendations of solicitors with regard to the form of reports, they should form their own independent views as to the opinions and contents expressed in their reports and exclude any suggestions which do not accord with their views.

15.3 Where experts change their opinion following a meeting of experts, a simple signed and dated addendum or memorandum to that effect is generally sufficient. In some cases, however, the benefit to the court of having an amended report may justify the cost of making the amendment.

15.4 Where experts significantly alter their opinion, as a result of new evidence or because evidence on which they relied has become unreliable, or for any other reason, they should amend their reports to reflect that fact. Amended reports should include reasons for amendments. In such circumstances those instructing experts should inform other parties as soon as possible of any change of opinion.

15.5 When experts intend to amend their reports, they should inform those instructing them without delay and give reasons. They should provide the amended version (or an addendum or memorandum) clearly marked as such as quickly as possible.

16. Written Questions to Experts

16.1 The procedure for putting written questions to experts (CPR 35.6) is intended to facilitate the clarification of opinions and issues after experts' reports have been served. Experts have a duty to provide answers to questions properly put. Where they fail to do so, the court may impose sanctions against the party instructing the expert, and, if, there is continued non-compliance, debar a party from relying on the report. Experts should copy their answers to those instructing them.

16.2 Experts' answers to questions automatically become part of their reports. They are covered by the statement of truth and form part of the expert evidence.

16.3 Where experts believe that questions put are not properly directed to the clarification of the report, or are disproportionate, or have been asked out of time, they should discuss the questions with those instructing them and, if appropriate, those asking the questions. Attempts should be made to resolve such problems without the need for an application to the court for directions.

Written requests for directions in relation to questions

16.4 If those instructing experts do not apply to the court in respect of questions, but experts still believe that questions are improper or out of time, experts may file written requests with the court for directions to assist in carrying out their functions as experts (CPR 35.14). See Section 11 above.

Ensuring questions have been 'properly put'

For a question to be properly put, it must conform to the requirements of Rule 35.6(2). Generally, it is for lawyers to decide whether a question meets the requirements, not experts. However, experts can avoid all possibility of censure for answering questions they ought not to have answered by relying on Rule 35.6(2)(ii). This permits any questions to be put (regardless of frequency, timing or purpose), providing all the parties agree.

If instructed by one party, an expert should send any questions he receives from another party to his instructing party and ask for permission to answer them. If permission is given, he will be covered by Rule 35.6(2)(ii).

A jointly instructed expert should only receive questions that have already been circulated to all parties, but he should nonetheless ensure all the parties agree to his answering any questions put to him.

17. Single Joint Experts

17.1 CPR 35 and PD35 deal extensively with the instruction and use of joint experts by the parties and the powers of the court to order their use (see CPR 35.7 and 35.8, PD35, para 5).

17.2 The Civil Procedure Rules encourage the use of joint experts. Wherever possible a joint report should be obtained. Consideration should therefore be given by all parties to the appointment of single joint experts in all cases where a court might direct such an appointment. Single joint experts are the norm in cases allocated to the small claims track and the fast track.

17.3 Where, in the early stages of a dispute, examinations, investigations, tests, site inspections, experiments, preparation of photographs, plans or other similar preliminary expert tasks are necessary, consideration should be given to the instruction of a single joint expert, especially where such matters are not, at that stage, expected to be contentious as between the parties. The objective of such an appointment should be to agree or to narrow issues.

17.5 Experts who have previously advised a party (whether in the same case or otherwise) should only be proposed as single joint experts if other parties are given all relevant information about the previous involvement.

17.6 The appointment of a single joint expert does not prevent parties from instructing their own experts to advise (but the costs of such expert advisors may not be recoverable in the case).

Joint instructions

17.7 The parties should try to agree joint instructions to single joint experts, but, in default of agreement, each party may give instructions. In particular, all parties should try to agree what documents should be included with instructions and what assumptions single joint experts should make.

17.8 Where the parties fail to agree joint instructions, they should try to agree where the areas of disagreement lie and their instructions should make this clear. If separate instructions are given, they should be copied at the same time to the other instructing parties.

17.9 Where experts are instructed by two or more parties, the terms of appointment should, unless the court has directed otherwise, or the parties have agreed otherwise, include:

(a) a statement that all the instructing parties are jointly and severally liable to pay the experts' fees and, accordingly, that experts' invoices should be sent simultaneously to all instructing parties or their solicitors (as appropriate); and

(b) a statement as to whether any order has been made limiting the amount of experts' fees and expenses [CPR 35.8(4)(a)].

17.10 Where instructions have not been received by the expert from one or more of the instructing parties the expert should give notice (normally at least 7 days) of a deadline to all instructing parties for the receipt by the expert of such instructions. Unless the instructions are received within the deadline the expert may begin work. In the event that instructions are received after the deadline but before the signing off of the report the expert should consider whether it is practicable to comply with those instructions without adversely affecting the timetable set for delivery of the report and in such a manner as to comply with the proportionality principle. An expert who decides to issue a report without taking into account instructions received after the deadline should inform the parties who may apply to the court for directions. In either event the report must show clearly that the expert did not receive instructions within the deadline, or, as the case may be, at all.

Conduct of the single joint expert

17.11 Single joint experts should keep all instructing parties informed of any material steps that they may be taking by, for example, copying all correspondence to those instructing them.

Avoid the telephone

If a jointly appointed expert is to avoid all possibility of censure, he would be wise to avoid all telephone contact with the parties, as the telephone tends to be bilateral in nature. Rely instead on written communication that can easily be copied to all parties simultaneously.

17.12 Single joint experts are Part 35 experts and so have an overriding duty to the court. They are the parties' appointed experts and therefore owe an equal duty to all parties. They should maintain independence, impartiality and transparency at all times.

17.13 Single joint experts should not attend any meeting or conference which is not a joint one, unless all the parties have agreed in writing or the court has directed that such a meeting may be held[4] and who is to pay the experts' fees for the meeting.

17.14 Single joint experts may request directions from the court – see Section 11 above.

17.15 Single joint experts should serve their reports simultaneously on all instructing parties. They should provide a single report even though they may have received instructions which contain areas of conflicting fact or allegation. If conflicting instructions lead to different opinions (for example, because the instructions require experts to make different assumptions of fact), reports may need to contain more than one set of opinions on any issue. It is for the court to determine the facts.

Cross-examination

17.16 Single joint experts do not normally give oral evidence at trial but if they do, all parties may cross-examine them. In general written questions (CPR 35.6) should be put to single joint experts before requests are made for them to attend court for the purpose of cross-examination.[5]

18. Discussions between Experts

18.1 The court has powers to direct discussions between experts for the purposes set out in the Rules (CPR 35.12). Parties may also agree that discussions take place between their experts.

---

[4] *Peet -v- Mid Kent Area Healthcare NHS Trust* [2002] 1 *WLR* 210.

[5] *Daniels -v- Walker* [2000] 1 *WLR* 1382.

18.2 Where single joint experts have been instructed but parties have, with the permission of the court, instructed their own additional Part 35 experts, there may, if the court so orders or the parties agree, be discussions between the single joint experts and the additional Part 35 experts. Such discussions should be confined to those matters within the remit of the additional Part 35 experts or as ordered by the court.

18.3 The purpose of discussions between experts should be, wherever possible, to:

(a) identify and discuss the expert issues in the proceedings;

(b) reach agreed opinions on those issues, and, if that is not possible, to narrow the issues in the case;

(c) identify those issues on which they agree and disagree and summarise their reasons for disagreement on any issue; and

(d) identify what action, if any, may be taken to resolve any of the outstanding issues between the parties.

The purpose is not negotiation

The purpose of discussions between experts is to identify, discuss and, where possible, agree opinion on expert issues. Experts should also seek to identify areas where their opinions differ, and give reasons for their disagreement. Experts should not treat the discussion as a negotiation. It is never acceptable for an expert to shift his opinion purely to obtain a concession from the other expert.

Arrangements for discussions between experts

18.4 Arrangements for discussions between experts should be proportionate to the value of cases. In small claims and fast-track cases there should not normally be meetings between experts. Where discussion is justified in such cases, telephone discussion or an exchange of letters should, in the interests of proportionality, usually suffice. In multi-track cases, discussion may be face to face, but the practicalities or the proportionality principle may require discussions to be by telephone or video conference.

18.5 The parties, their lawyers and experts should co-operate to produce the agenda for any discussion between experts, although primary responsibility for preparation of the agenda should normally lie with the parties' solicitors.

18.6 The agenda should indicate what matters have been agreed and summarise concisely those which are in issue. It is often helpful for it to include questions to be answered by the experts. If agreement cannot be reached promptly or a party is unrepresented, the court may give directions for the drawing up of the agenda. The agenda should be circulated to experts and those instructing them to allow sufficient time for the experts to prepare for the discussion.

18.7 Those instructing experts must not instruct experts to avoid reaching agreement (or to defer doing so) on any matter within the experts' competence. Experts are not permitted to accept such instructions.

18.8 The parties' lawyers may only be present at discussions between experts if all the parties agree or the court so orders. If lawyers do attend, they should not normally intervene except to answer questions put to them by the experts or to advise about the law.[6]

18.9 The content of discussions between experts should not be referred to at trial unless the parties agree [CPR 35.12(4)]. It is good practice for any such agreement to be in writing.

18.10 At the conclusion of any discussion between experts, a statement should be prepared setting out:

(a)   a list of issues that have been agreed, including, in each instance, the basis of agreement;

(b)   a list of issues that have not been agreed, including, in each instance, the basis of disagreement;

(c)   a list of any further issues that have arisen that were not included in the original agenda for discussion;

(d)   a record of further action, if any, to be taken or recommended, including as appropriate the holding of further discussions between experts.

18.11 The statement should be agreed and signed by all the parties to the discussion as soon as may be practicable.

18.12 Agreements between experts during discussions do not bind the parties unless the parties expressly agree to be bound by the agreement [CPR 35.12(5)]. However, in view of the overriding objective, parties should give careful consideration before refusing to be bound by such an agreement and be able to explain their refusal should it become relevant to the issue of costs.

19. Attendance of Experts at Court

19.1 Experts instructed in cases have an obligation to attend court if called upon to do so and accordingly should ensure that those instructing them are always aware of their dates to be avoided and take all reasonable steps to be available.

19.2 Those instructing experts should:

(a)   ascertain the availability of experts before trial dates are fixed;

---

[6] *Hubbard -v- Lambeth, Southwark & Lewisham HA* [2001] *EWCA Civ* 1455.

(b) keep experts updated with timetables (including the dates and times experts are to attend) and the location of the court;

(c) give consideration, where appropriate, to experts giving evidence via a video-link;

(d) inform experts immediately if trial dates are vacated.

19.3 Experts should normally attend court without the need for the service of witness summonses, but on occasion they may be served to require attendance (CPR 34). The use of witness summonses does not affect the contractual or other obligations of the parties to pay experts' fees.

Appendix 4: Cresswell and Toulmin

The principles of expert evidence which Mr Justice Cresswell laid down in his judgment in the shipping case known as *The Ikarian Reefer*[7] have become widely accepted as a classic statement of the duties and responsibilities of expert witnesses. They were endorsed by the Court of Appeal, commended by Lord Woolf in his report on the civil justice system in England and Wales, and have been cited with approval in several subsequent cases. This is not to say, though, that they have won complete acceptance, as the following discussion shows. It is based on an article by Anthony Speaight QC, which first appeared in the *New Law Journal* and was then abridged, with the author's permission, for publication in *Your Witness*.

Cresswell Principles

The seven principles of expert evidence which Mr Justice Cresswell set out in *The Ikarian Reefer* have several times been cited as the classic statement of good practice for experts. There can be no doubt that the judge's strictures on experts in this case were justified. But before the *Ikarian Reefer* principles become, so to speak, set in stone as unchallengeable pillars of wisdom, we ought to examine the respects in which they may fail to grapple with unresolved contradictions in the role of the expert in litigation. Let us consider the principles individually.

1. Expert evidence presented to the court should be, and should be seen to be, the independent product of the expert uninfluenced as to form or content by the exigencies of litigation.

If this simply meant that an expert ought to express the same opinion on a given issue irrespective of which side was calling him, then most of us would warmly agree. However, in stating that both 'form and content' should be uninfluenced by 'the exigencies of litigation' the proposition goes much further.

Consider form first. How can an expert report not be influenced by the fact that it is to be used in litigation? Litigation reports differ from those produced for other purposes in a number of ways, most importantly because they should surely be directed to the matters in issue on which expert evidence is admissible. In my view it is not only proper but desirable for lawyers to identify for experts the issues on which their opinion is sought. To my mind, a crisp expert report will set out the questions posed by the lawyers and confine itself to answering them. Therefore, the form of a

---

[7] *National Justice Compania Naviera SA -v- Prudential Assurance Company Ltd (Ikarian Reefer)* [1993] 2 *Lloyd's Rep* 68.

useful expert report will be very much dictated by the context of its requirement for a particular case.

The proposition that the content of the report should be uninfluenced by the exigencies of litigation may sound more reasonable. But, in fact, behind this bland statement lies a profound difference of opinion as to the propriety of lawyer involvement in the drafting of reports. Imagine the hypothetical case of an obstetrician accused of pulling too hard on forceps. The defendants receive a report from their medical expert which contains these two passages: (1) 'in my opinion he did not pull too hard but he did pull for too long, and this ultimately produced the same mischief as pulling too hard would have done', and (2) 'in the ensuing Caesarean section operation his stitching was thoroughly careless, causing unnecessary later pain'.

In my view it would be wrong for a lawyer to suggest that passage (1) be modified by, for example, cutting out all the words after 'he did not pull too hard'; for such an excision would do violence to the witness's full expression of opinion on the question as to whether the pulling was negligent. On the other hand, I would consider it perfectly proper for a lawyer to ask the expert to omit passage (2) entirely if the plaintiff had pleaded no allegation of negligence in the performance of the later operation. Parties to litigation are under no obligation to tell their opponents how they could improve their cases, and in such a situation it would be the lawyer's duty to his client to endeavour to have passage (2) removed before the report was served.

Therefore, to the extent that the content of expert reports should be confined to the questions posed to the expert, the content as well as the form may on occasions be influenced by the requirements of litigation.

2. An expert witness should provide independent assistance to the court by way of objective unbiased opinion in relation to matters within his expertise (see Polivitte Ltd -v- Commercial Union Assurance). An expert witness in the High Court should never assume the role of an advocate.

Experts should certainly provide objective unbiased opinions, and equally certainly they should not act as advocates. However, the giving of unbiased opinions is not quite the same thing as providing 'independent assistance to the court'. Experts are called by one party or the other, and are paid by one of the parties. They are engaged not only to give evidence in the witness box, but also to give out-of-court advice to the party engaging them. And, indeed, on looking at Mr Justice Garland's judgment in the Polivitte case one finds that he gave a rather more balanced picture of the expert's role: 'I have almost considered the role of an expert to be two-fold: first, to advance the case of the party calling him, so far as it can properly be advanced on the basis of information available to the expert in the professional exercise of his skill and experience; and secondly, to assist the court, which does not possess the relevant skill and experience, in determining where the truth lies.'

3. An expert witness should state the facts or assumptions upon which his opinion is based. He should not omit to consider material facts which could detract from his concluded opinion.

This statement is fine, so long as the reference to not omitting what could detract from the opinion is limited to the questions actually posed to the expert. As the late and greatly respected Official Referee, Judge John Newey QC, once wrote: 'Since the procedure in both courts and arbitrations is adversarial, an expert is not obliged to speak out, or write in his report, about matters concerning which he has not been asked.'

4. An expert witness should make it clear when a particular question or issue falls outside his expertise.

When *The Ikarian Reefer* case reached the Court of Appeal, Lord Justice Stuart-Smith qualified this statement from the judgment of the Divisional Court by saying that an experienced fire expert must be entitled to weigh the probabilities. 'This', he said, 'may involve making use of the skills of other experts or drawing on his general mechanical or chemical knowledge.'

5. If an expert's opinion is not properly researched because he considers that insufficient data are available, then this must be stated with an indication that the opinion is no more than provisional. In cases where an expert witness who has prepared a report could not assert that the report contained the truth, the whole truth and nothing but the truth without some qualification, that qualification should be stated in the report (see Derby -v- Weldon).

The remarks of Lord Justice Staughton in the *Derby -v- Weldon* case are worth quoting more fully, because they introduce a different, and more realistic, nuance: 'I do not think that an expert witness, or any other witness, obliges himself to volunteer his views on every issue in the whole case when he takes an oath to tell the whole truth. What he does oblige himself to do is to tell the whole truth about those matters which he is asked about.'

6. If, after exchange of reports, an expert witness changes his view on a material matter having read the other side's expert's report or for any other reason, such a change of view should be communicated (through legal representatives) to the other side without delay and when appropriate to the court.

This is a radical idea. I have never had the experience of opponents telling me or my solicitors that their expert had changed his view on something since service of his report. Nor have I ever heard of it happening to others. So this principle hardly reflects existing practice. That is not to say that there may not be good arguments in favour of its adoption, but they require careful examination.

In general, a party to litigation is under no obligation to reveal to the other what his prospective witnesses will say. Quite the contrary: witness statements are privileged. However, rules of court have in practice modified the scope of that privilege, by providing that leave to call experts may be made conditional on the substance of their evidence being disclosed to the other side in the form of a written report.

I can quite see that if an expert changed his mind on a significant matter between writing his report and its service to the other side, the report should be amended before it is served. It could well be argued that service implies that the report currently reflects the witness's view, even if the report had been completed some time previously. Similarly, I would agree that a party ought not to place an expert's report before the trial judge unless at the time of doing so the report is still broadly accurate as to the witness's opinions, and the party genuinely intends to call that expert.

But no recipient of a report could imagine that it constituted the author's final views on the subject, for no author can predict how his opinions may change in the future, especially if additional material comes to his attention. So if an expert changes his mind on a matter during the many months that may elapse between service of his report and trial, is there any obligation to signal that to the other side? I think not, and other lawyers share my view.

7. Where expert evidence refers to photographs, plans, calculations, analyses, measurements, survey reports or other similar documents, these must be provided to the opposite party at the same time as the exchange of reports.

A good statement of practice.

Anthony Speaight, QC

The Toulmin Principles

Seven years after Mr Justice Cresswell formulated the above principles of expert evidence, a judge in the Technology and Construction Court, Judge John Toulmin CMG, QC, had occasion to update them in the light of the Woolf reforms. The details of the case Judge Toulmin was trying, *Anglo Group plc -v- Winther Brown & Co. Ltd and BML (Office Computers) Ltd*, need not concern us here, but his restatement of the 'Cresswell principles' has relevance for all who practice as expert witnesses.

Judge Toulmin was highly critical of some of the expert evidence he had heard in the case. But before dealing with it in his judgment, he listed the following as duties an expert witness owes to the court:

'1. An expert witness should at all stages in the procedure, on the basis of the evidence as he understands it, provide independent assistance to the court and the parties by way of objective unbiased opinion in relation to matters within his expertise. This applies as much to the initial meetings of experts as to evidence at trial. An expert should never assume the role of an advocate.

'2. The expert's evidence should normally be confined to technical matters on which the court will be assisted by receiving an explanation, or to evidence of common professional practice. The expert witness should not give evidence or opinions as to what the expert himself would have done in similar circumstances or otherwise seek to usurp the role of the judge.

'3. He should co-operate with the expert of the other party or parties in attempting to narrow the technical issues in dispute at the earliest possible stage of the procedure and to eliminate or place in context any peripheral issues. He should co-operate with the other expert(s) in attending without-prejudice meetings as necessary and in seeking to find areas of agreement and to define precisely areas of disagreement to be set out in the joint statement of experts ordered by the court.

'4. The expert evidence presented to the court should be, and be seen to be, the independent product of the expert uninfluenced as to form or content by the exigencies of the litigation.

'5. An expert witness should state the facts or assumptions upon which his opinion is based. He should not omit to consider material facts which could detract from his concluded opinion.

'6. An expert witness should make it clear when a particular question or issue falls outside his expertise.

'7. Where an expert is of the opinion that his conclusions are based on inadequate factual information he should say so explicitly.

'8. An expert should be ready to reconsider his opinion and, if appropriate, to change his mind when he has received new information or has considered the opinion of the other expert. He should do so at the earliest opportunity.'

Glossary and Abbreviations

AC *Law Reports: Appeal Cases*

Action Legal proceedings in the civil justice system

Advocate A lawyer who pleads the case for a party. Advocates are supposed to be partisan, putting forward the best possible case for the party. **Expert witnesses are not advocates.**

AER *All England Law Reports*

Assessment The process by which the court decides the amount of legal costs to be paid between the parties. This does not affect the fees due to an expert witness, unless he has agreed *at the outset* to have his fee subject to assessment.

Burden of proof The burden of proof falls on the party that has to prove its case. Compare with **Standard of proof**.

BLR *Business Law Review*

Case management Decisions taken by the court controlling how an action progresses

Ch *Law Reports: Chancery Division*

CJC Civil Justice Council

Claimant The person making the claim – previously known as the plaintiff

Claim form The document that starts a civil action

Conduct money The money paid on service of a witness summons for the cost of travel to court and any loss of income

CPR Civil Procedure Rules

CP *Law Reports: Common Pleas*

CRFP Council for the Registration of Forensic Practitioners

Damages Money paid as compensation

DCA Department for Constitutional Affairs (formerly the Lord Chancellor's Department)

EG *Estates Gazette*

EHRR *European Human Rights Reports*

EWCA Civ *Court of Appeal for England & Wales, Civil Division*

EWCA Crim *Court of Appeal for England & Wales, Criminal Division*

Fast track The CPR case management track dealing mostly with claims valued between £5,000 and £15,000

FSR *Fleet Street Reports*

GMC General Medical Council

Lloyd's Rep *Lloyd's Reports*

LSC Legal Services Commission

Med LR *Medical Law Reports*

Multi-track The CPR case management track dealing mostly with large or complex claims valued over £15,000

Obiter dicta The observations made in the course of a judgment which are not necessary in reaching the decision. This is the opposite of the *ratio decedendi* in a case, or the 'reason for deciding'.

Party One of the sides in a case, i.e. claimant or defendant

Pleadings The collective term for the written statements delivered by parties to one another setting out the legal and factual basis of a claim or defence. Pleadings may include a statement of claim, defence, counter-claim or reply.

Pre-action protocol Guidance associated with the CPR which seeks to extend the open approach of the CPR into the handling of cases before proceedings are actually issued

Quantum The value of a claim in monetary terms

RPC *Reports of Patent Cases*

Settlement An agreement by the parties to end a case without going to court

Small claims track The CPR case management track dealing with claims valued below £5,000. Most of the CPR requirements for expert evidence do not apply for cases on this track.

Standard of proof The level of proof that must be shown by a party for the court to rule in its favour. In civil cases, the standard of proof is normally 'on the balance of probabilities'.

Statement of case The formal court document setting out each party's case.

Summary judgment A judgment given by a civil court without holding a full hearing

TLR *Times Law Reports*

Tort A civil wrong (independent of contract) giving rise to a cause of action

Without prejudice Without loss of any rights. Communications capable of attracting privilege and marked 'without prejudice' cannot be used in evidence in court proceedings.

Witness summons A written order of a court requiring the attendance of a witness at court. Non-compliance is a contempt of court which may result in imprisonment. Previously known as a *subpeona*.

WLR *Weekly Law Reports*

Index